EL SALVADOR

EL SALVADOR

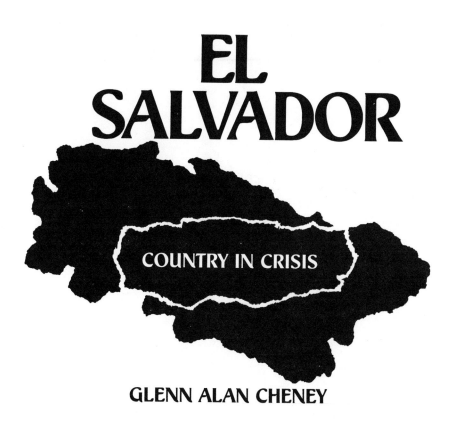

COUNTRY IN CRISIS

GLENN ALAN CHENEY

An Impact Book • Revised Edition • 1990
Franklin Watts
New York • London • Toronto • Sydney

Map by: Joe Le Monnier
Photographs courtesy of: Woodfin Camp: pp. 12 (Paulo Texeira/
Lehtikuva Oy), 63 (Bob Nicklesberg), 76, 84, 86 (all Alon Reininger/
Contact), 111 (Paolo Texeira/rs), 113 (Bob Nicklesberg); Impact
Visuals: pp. 21, 24, 28, 67 (all Donna De Cesare), 47, 77 (Rick
Reinhard), 79 (Steve Cagan), 118 (Les Stone); UPI/Bettmann: pp.
41, 55, 59, 70, 74, 102; Liaison: p. 93 (Markel).

Library of Congress Cataloging-in-Publication Data
Cheney, Glenn Alan.
El Salvador / by Glenn Alan Cheney.— 2nd ed.
p.   cm. —(An Impact book)
Rev. ed. of: El Salvador, country in crisis. 1982.
Summary: examines the political and social situation in El
Salvador, with an emphasis on the recent civil war and its impact
on living conditions throughout the country.
ISBN 0-531-10916-X
1. El Salvador—Politics and government—1979—Juvenile
literature. 2. El Salvador—Politics and government—1944-1979—
Juvenile literature. 3. Government, Resistance to—El Salvador—
History—20th century—Juvenile literature. 4. El Salvador—
Relations—United States—Juvenile literature. 5. United States—
Relations—El Salvador—Juvenile literature. [1. El Salvador—
Politics and government.] I. Cheney, Glenn Alan. El Salvador,
country in crisis. II. Title.
F1488.3.C47   1990
972.8405'3—dc20   89-38708   CIP   AC

Also by Glenn Alan Cheney

Mineral Resources
Responsibility
Revolution in Central America

*Dedicated to
Oscar Arnulfo Romero,
Archbishop
of El Salvador*

CONTENTS

EL SALVADOR

INTRODUCTION

Over the past few years, El Salvador has literally fought its way into the headlines of newspapers all over the world. Once a small and easily ignorable Central American country, El Salvador has taken on pivotal importance in international politics. To Americans, it is a critical point in an ever-evolving foreign policy.

The fighting is the ugliest kind of conflict—a civil war in which Salvadorans are killing Salvadorans. Guerrilla armies of impoverished peasants are battling military forces that operate beyond effective government control. The guerrillas assassinate government officials and rich landowners; the army kills and tortures innocent peasants; death squads roam at will. Between the various forces, over 70,000 people have died, though nine-tenths of them had little or nothing to do with the war.

The shock waves of the conflict reach around the globe. Many governments consider the guerrillas communists, and there is evidence that communist countries

are supplying their arms and ammunition. Other governments say that the Salvadoran political system is a repressive military dictatorship and its socioeconomic system is feudalistic. The people and leaders of the United States are divided as both sides of the issue have valid points.

With the full support of the U.S. government, El Salvador is trying a bold and historically unique solution to the problem. Under a program of sweeping land reform, hundreds of farms have been taken from the rich and distributed among the poor. The hope is that this will put the people's support behind the government instead of behind the guerrillas. Whether this land reform is working remains hotly debated and highly unproven.

The issue for the United States is how this country should interpret and react to this complex conflict. Is the Salvadoran government really trying to become a democracy or is it a persistently military regime? Are the guerrillas truly supported by foreign powers? Is land reform a solution to peasant uprising? Should the U.S. support the Salvadoran government, and if so, how? With troops? Weapons? Economic aid?

A powerful symbol
of the strife and
conflict in El Salvador.
This ten-year-old
boy is housed at a
military headquarters.
He is holding a U.S.-
made rifle. Both the
guerrillas and the
Salvadoran army
recruit young boys.

The answers to these questions are important not only for El Salvador today but for other countries tomorrow as well. As the U.S. and the Soviet Union engage in a contest for friends and influence around the world, the policies of the present are crucial to the future. This is no time for mistakes. An in-depth understanding of the circumstances is essential to the United States, to El Salvador, and to the countries of Latin America.

1

THE SOCIAL DILEMMA

The people of El Salvador are fighting for freedom, power, money, justice, and vengeance. But all these points of conflict revolve around a single question: Who should own the land?

As the smallest and most densely populated mainland country in the Western Hemisphere, El Salvador does not have sufficient land to support its people. It is about the size and shape of Massachusetts—a 160-mile-long (257 km) rectangle of about 8,260 square miles (21,400 sq km). Its population is almost as large as that of Massachusetts, too. Estimates vary from 5 to 6 million. The population growth rate, 3.5 percent, is one of the fastest in Latin America.

The average population density is more than 600 people per square mile. Sixty percent of these people live in the rural areas outside the cities and towns. For an agricultural country that has no oil, no mineral deposits, no natural resources, and little industry, this overpopulation can be disastrous. Massachusetts, with a similar

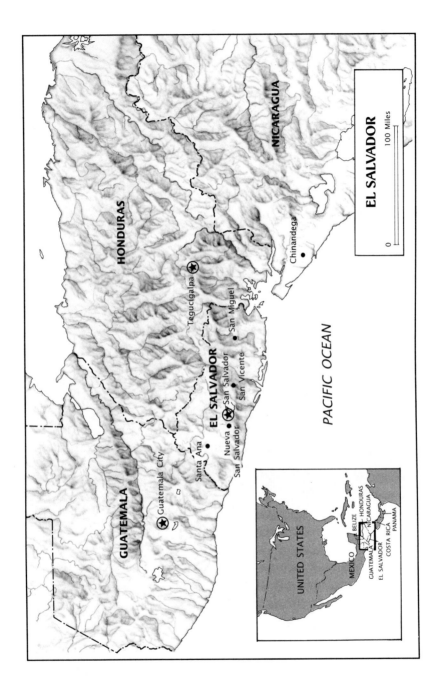

EL SALVADOR

0   100 Miles

GUATEMALA

HONDURAS

NICARAGUA

EL SALVADOR

PACIFIC OCEAN

Guatemala City

Santa Ana

Nueva
San Salvador

San Salvador

San Vicente

San Miguel

Tegucigalpa

Chinandega

UNITED STATES

MEXICO

BELIZE

GUATEMALA

EL SALVADOR

HONDURAS

NICARAGUA

COSTA RICA

PANAMA

population density, can import food from fertile and spacious farming states like Kansas and Iowa, where there are fewer than 50 people per square mile. The people of El Salvador must grow what they eat or import it at great expense.

Fortunately, most of the terrain is good for farming. The ragged Sierra Madre mountains lie to the north, in Honduras, so El Salvador, on the Pacific side of the Central American isthmus, enjoys gentle foothills as well as protection from the hurricanes that ravage the Caribbean coast.

El Salvador's many volcanoes (more than any other Latin American country; four are still active) provide perfect soil for growing coffee. The roots of the coffee trees, which hold the soil in place, thrive on the volcanic pumice and ash. In addition, the slight altitude of the country, between 2,000 and 3,000 feet (610 to 914 m) above sea level, keeps the air comfortably cool for the plants and the people who tend them. Temperatures average 75°F (24°C), and about 70 inches (178 cm) of rain fall every year.

Temperatures vary with altitude rather than latitude. Along the coast, the climate is tropical, with an average temperature of 80.2°F (27°C) and 85 inches (216 cm) of rainfall per year. Here and in the low inland valleys, cotton and sugarcane are the principal crops. The exportation of these crops, together with coffee, provides El Salvador with more than 70 percent of its income.

The country's seasons are divided into rainy and dry. From May to October, the rains are torrential most of the time. Though these are actually summer months, Salvadorans call this time of year winter because of the lower temperatures and bone-chilling humidity. When the weather is drier and warmer, from October to May, workers harvest the coffee, cotton, and sugarcane.

Crops for Cash • Most of the best land in El Salvador is devoted to *cash crops*—coffee, cotton, and sugarcane, which are grown to sell to other countries. Only a small portion is consumed in El Salvador. Because cash crops are worth so much more than food crops, it is more economical to grow them and use the profits to import food from neighboring countries.

Most cash crops are grown on tracts of land of more than 40 hectares (100 acres). Coffee, the most profitable, grows on medium-sized farms (of 100 to 300 hectares, or 250 to 750 acres) and provides El Salvador with 50 percent of its income from exports. Though cultivation costs are low and the selling price is high, the production of coffee demands an initial investment of five years, the time it takes a coffee tree to mature and bear beans. In the 1960s El Salvador became the world's highest-yielding coffee producer, growing an average of 770 pounds per acre, almost double the yield of most other countries. Its biggest customers are the United States and West Germany.

Cotton is cultivated on the hot, wet plantations along the coast and in some low-lying valleys in the interior. Enormous tracts of land are required, for cotton is a profitable crop only if great quantities are produced. The expense of shipping the crop by truck or train to the textile mills in the capital city, San Salvador, or to one of the three major Pacific ports, La Unión, La Libertad, or Acajutla, is considerable. Most raw cotton and fabric are shipped to Japan.

Sugarcane grows on plateaus and in inland valleys that are too high for cotton. This crop is profitable for the businessman/farmer who owns the fields, has installed mechanized planting and harvesting processes, and has business interests in sugar refineries.

Crops for Food • Farmers who do not have enough land to grow cash crops engage in *subsistence farming*. They raise food crops only for themselves and their families. At best, they may have a bit left over to sell at the market.

Maize, a miraculously sturdy breed of corn, is the staple of subsistence farmers. It can grow anywhere there is soil—around houses, along roads, in clearings, and even on the sides of cliffs. It needs no fertilizer and can survive excessive rainfalls and droughts. The more profitable hybrid corns are grown only by those who can afford fertilizer, irrigation, and the possible loss of a crop as a result of excessively wet or dry weather.

Beans and sorghum are also important to the subsistence farmer. The beans are dried and stored all winter, and the sorghum is used not only to fatten chickens and livestock, but also to make the tortillas that are a staple of the Salvadoran diet. Beans and sorghum are often planted between rows of corn.

On land not good enough for crops, especially the dry lands of the north, Salvadorans raise cattle and hogs. There are a few large cattle ranches, and beef exports have been increasing. Most hogs are raised by individual families for personal consumption.

Almost 40 percent of El Salvador can be easily farmed, and all of that land is occupied. With so much acreage devoted to cash crops, until recently El Salvador's income as a nation has exceeded that of most of its Central American neighbors. In tragic contradiction, however, the majority of its people survive on a level of near starvation.

In a country where agriculture constitutes 25 percent of the gross national product, employs 60 percent of the population, and brings in 90 percent of the country's income from exports, the concentration of land in a few hands creates extremes of wealth and poverty. Those with great tracts of land can generate tremendous wealth, and those with little or no land earn no more than minimum wages. The gap between the extremes of wealth and poverty results in distinct upper and lower classes with only a small middle class between.

The Upper Class • Until March 1980, well over half the land in El Salvador belonged to just 2 percent of the population—the wealthy and politically powerful upper class. Until then they also owned the banks that lent money for fertilizer, seed, and farm development, and they controlled the export companies that sold and shipped cash crops all over the world.

Despite the changes that came with the land reform act in 1980, this upper class of 300 families of distant cousins and in-laws has continued cooperating to keep the nation's wealth in their hands. They still own most of the land, as well as the trucks and railroads that transport crops and the refineries and mills that buy sugar and cotton.

This is the healthy and educated class. They can afford to stay in private hospitals or even fly to the United States for medical care. Their children go to private schools in San Salvador and to college in the United States or Europe. By the time they are adults, they are well prepared for the eventual ownership of their parents' farms and businesses.

The upper-class homes, situated in well-guarded sections of San Salvador, are equipped with everything from French food processors and American vacuum cleaners to Japanese stereos and color television sets. With the help of a maid or two, the housewife has time for social activities and the further education of her children with piano, ballet, English, and other private lessons.

The typical upper-class family also has a large house on the farm. If the farm is near San Salvador, the owners may commute there on weekends, perhaps by private plane. Otherwise they stay on the farm only during harvest

Homes of the upper class are all hidden behind
high walls and gates. Yet the reality of poverty
is never far away. On some upper-class streets,
poor squatters also live. Generally, they live
in the ditches along the sewage rivers that flow
away from the hills of the rich homes.

time to help the resident administrator oversee this critical operation. Because most farming business involves banks and transport and export companies, the owner spends more time in offices in the capital than in the fields of his farm.

Over the past fifty years the families of the upper class have greatly increased their landholdings and have used the land to increase their wealth. That wealth has given them the means literally to buy political power by financially influencing the armed forces that control the government. With this power, they have enforced a political structure that facilitates the further accumulation of land and wealth. This one-way flow of money and power is a principal cause of the present political problems of El Salvador.

The Lower Class • The increase in the size of farms of the large landowners has been at the expense of the Salvadoran peasants, who are called *campesinos*. The life-style of the large and ever-increasing lower class stands in stark contrast to that of the upper class.

As the *campesinos* lost land to the large landowners, they also lost the means of making the money they needed to improve and hold on to what little land they had left. The harder it became for the poor to keep their land, the easier it became for the wealthy to buy it up. As the gap between rich and poor widened, the movement to greater class extremes accelerated toward absolutely invulnerable wealth and totally inescapable poverty.

A baby born into the lower class faces a dismal future. He or she may not live a year, for 63 out of 1,000 peasant babies do not (compared to fewer than 20 per 1,000 in the United States). To the peasant baby, the future means hunger, for 75 percent of peasants under the age of five are malnourished. Of all deaths in El Salvador, 45 percent occur in childhood, the result of infant mortality, childhood diseases, and malnourishment.

The *campesinos* lack education as well as health care. Only 50 percent of the children may learn to read and write; even fewer will finish the fourth grade. There is almost no hope of finishing high school or going to college.

The *campesinos*, who make up about 60 percent of El Salvador's population, are cast into three levels of poverty: subsistence farmers; *colonos*, who live on the farms where they are employed; and *jornaleros*, or migrant workers.

Subsistence farmers still own or are able to rent a bit of land. They are the most privileged of the poor. The average subsistence farmer has a two- or three-room house of mud walls, packed-earth floors, and a thatched or corrugated metal roof. Because the land is usually not adequate to supply food for a whole year, let alone any extra to sell for money to buy clothes, tools, medicines, and household goods, the father of the family may spend four or five months of the year traveling to the larger farms where he can earn wages during harvest. Subsistence farmers and their families consume a simple diet. Pancake-shaped tortillas made of ground maize are a part of every meal. Wrapped around the homegrown beans and perhaps a bit of pork or hard-boiled egg, this Salvadoran sandwich barely provides enough nutrients to maintain health.

If the farmer rents the land he tills, it is probably through a sharecropping agreement under which he pays rent with part of his crops. Sometimes the portion he must pay is as much as half of what he grows.

The *colonos* are a slightly lower, but still privileged, level of the poor. Originally, *colonos* were families allowed to live in a small house, called a *mesón*, on a large

Thousands of shacks crowd this wretched area of San Salvador. This particular community has more than 25,000 inhabitants and more than 11,000 of them are children. Most of the people are unemployed.

cash-crop plantation. The owner provided the house and the land around it to assure himself of a local labor supply. The *colonos* could till the land around the house and use either crops or labor to pay their rent.

Recently, though, with the rising value of land for cash crops, the area adjacent to the *mesón* has been devoted totally to the owner's crops, and the *mesónes* have become housing for transient, wage-earning laborers, not permanent subsistence farmers. Rather than a single home, the *mesón* is now a long row of back-to-back rooms with one family living in each room, which has a door but no window. Cooking is done outside. One latrine and probably perhaps a shower house serve everyone, and they all share a common spigot for drinking water. If they are lucky, each room has an electric light hanging from the ceiling.

The most fortunate *colonos* are those who work all year. Coffee trees need pruning, raking, and other care. Cotton and sugarcane farms need work done on machinery, irrigation, and general maintenance. But because wages are generally lower between harvests, many *colonos*, unable to earn enough to pay the rent, are forced to move on.

The descent in status from *colono* to migrant worker is becoming more and more frequent in El Salvador. The country's exploding population and the disappearance of available land has left more than half the rural population with nowhere to live, nowhere to find regular year-round work, and no way to raise or buy food. As a result, migrant workers are the poorest of the poor. They are able to earn wages only during harvest and planting seasons, and even then they are not able to earn very much. Because more than 40 percent of the rural population is now considered unnecessary for the planting and harvesting of crops, the large landowners have no reason to pay more than a bare minimum of about $5.70 per day. If a worker does not like the offered wages, the landowner can find a replacement among the thousands who are looking for work.

During the rainy season there is no work for the migrants. They live as squatters in temporary shelters on public land and along roads. Their houses are often no more than packing crates or cardboard lean-tos. Having nothing to lose, they may try squatting on plantation land until off-duty soldiers, hired to patrol private property, run them off.

As they wait out the long, damp winter, their possessions and food supplies rot with mold and mildew. After a few months, survival depends on whatever they can find growing, perhaps a secret patch of maize planted in May.

Wet and malnourished, cold if in the highlands or infested with insects if in the coastal lowlands, many die of pneumonia or tuberculosis, and infant mortality soars. Medical care is rarely available, and when it is, there is a long line to wait in.

When the rains stop, the harvest begins. The radio stations announce where migrants may go for work. They arrive, individually or in families, with little more than blankets and empty stomachs. Because the *mesón* has room for only a few families, many sleep outdoors on the ground. On coffee plantations in the hills, the nights are cool. Migrants coming up from the coast are especially uncomfortable, and respiratory diseases are common. Gastrointestinal ailments, the most prevalent diseases in Central America, attack everyone's stomach and intestines; few *campesinos* do not have some form of dysentery.

The Middle Class • In more industrially developed countries, the people of the lower class often have an opportunity to climb out of their poverty by working their way into the middle class. The middle class acts as a kind of protective buffer zone between the poor and the rich. The realistic possibility of rising toward relative wealth gives the poor hope and an alternative to violent reaction against the upper class.

In El Salvador the middle class is a very narrow buffer zone. Located almost entirely in San Salvador, it is not much larger than the upper class. Ranging from upper-middle to lower-middle class, these people are doctors and dentists, teachers and university professors, shop owners and small businessmen, office and factory workers. Most members of the middle class can afford medical care and at least a high school education for their children. Their homes of four or five rooms have the basic amenities of plumbing and electricity, and owning a car might be within their means.

The middle class emerged relatively recently in Salvadoran history. With the coming of industry in the 1960s, a few poor people from the farms managed to get factory jobs in San Salvador. These jobs became stepping-stones into the middle class. With regular year-round wages and the availability of schools, children had a chance to finish high school and learn the skills that allowed them to earn more than the minimum wage. Once over this hurdle, the family had some hope for the future. The middle class has not expanded much, however, because the population has grown faster than industry, and few additional jobs in factories have opened up.

The Urban Poor • Hoping to find factory jobs, hundreds of thousands of landless *campesinos* flocked to the capital in the 1960s. But the population quickly exceeded the available openings. Between the high birthrate and the sudden immigration, the population of San Salvador rose

by about 50 percent between 1961 and 1971, but the number of manufacturing jobs rose by only 6 percent. Consequently, slums of metal and scrap-lumber shacks now perch on the sides of steep hills and on the banks of the deep gullies that cut through San Salvador. Sixty percent of the capital's houses are not connected to the city sewer system, and only 30 percent have drinking water available. Violent crime, alcoholism, divorce, and the abandonment of families are all high. Rather than attend the overcrowded and understaffed public schools, children wander the streets in search of menial jobs. Often, because their poor families offer little reason to stay at home, children become independent before they are ten years old. The plight of the urban poor is just as hopeless as that of the landless *campesino*. Today, thousands flee the fighting in the rural areas. The number of homeless people in San Salvador has increased, as has their suffering.

The Problem of Illiteracy • With an illiteracy rate of 70 percent, *campesinos* and urban poor alike are trapped in a vicious circle. Because they have no education, they cannot work their way out of the lower class. Yet because they are in the lower class, they have trouble getting an education.

People living in this urban area cannot afford to rent one of the apartments in the building in the background. The apartments cost about $60.00 a month, but the average earnings among these people is about $6.00 per week.

Children must begin contributing to the family income at a young age. For the *campesinos*, this means working in the fields with their parents. As the family migrates between harvests and squats on land far from village schools, the children can never complete several years of education. At an average per capita income of only $133 per year, the rural poor never have enough money to settle down near any of the few schools in the rural areas.

The large landowners, who control the government, have done little to encourage the education of the lower class. For them, a surplus of illiterate workers means plenty of cheap and obedient labor for their farms.

Government by the Few • Politically, the government of El Salvador is an oligarchy, a system in which power is concentrated in the hands of a few people—in this case, the small group of upper-class landowners. This minority controls the country's government by its pervasive influence on the military forces, which are, in turn, responsible for governing the people.

Since 1932, all Salvadoran presidents have been army officers. With their wealth, the oligarchy can secretly pay army officers and other government officials to preserve the system by suppressing all political parties that want change. The officials are also rewarded for prohibiting strikes and union activity and for keeping the minimum wage as low as possible. A president who changes the laws to the detriment of the upper class faces the risk of being overthrown by a group of officers who find themselves the new recipients of the oligarchy's financial support.

Upper-class control of the military also reaches local military commanders, who are often little more than the private police force of the local landowners. They can be called upon to arrest squatters, union leaders, and other troublemakers. The bribes paid to the commanders are filtered down through the ranks, ensuring their cooperation in future operations. *Campesinos* daring to complain about the system or a personal injustice are not able to find a judge to listen to them, and they are usually arrested, if not killed outright.

The lack of land, the class division, the poverty, the hopelessness, and the injustices of a military regime all combine to drive the *campesinos* to the brink of violent reaction. When their frustrations become intolerable and they have nothing else to lose, many of the poor take up arms and risk their lives in a desperate attempt to somehow change the situation.

2

A HISTORY OF REPRESSION

The two sides fighting in El Salvador are often referred to by various names: left and right, liberal and conservative, Marxist, communist, socialist, and capitalist. Defining these terms is difficult because they are all relative and depend on one's point of view. Labeling individuals or organizations is difficult because it calls for generalizations that can lead to inaccuracies.

In general, though, *leftists* are those who lean toward the Marxist beliefs of communism and socialism. There are *extreme leftists*, also called *Marxists*, who advocate a strong Soviet or Cuban style of communism. *Moderate leftists* tend to want a democracy and a milder form of socialism. A *liberal* is anyone who wants a change toward the left, however slight. In El Salvador, a liberal is one advocating social-improvement programs or more freedom for the poor.

On the other end of the political spectrum are the *rightists*. Advocating capitalism, they want little or no government control of business, industry, or the economy. *Extreme rightists* want a strong government that will use force to repress those who want to change the present system. A *conservative* is anyone who does not want to change the present system.

Between the left and the right stand the *moderates*, or *centrists*. In general, they advocate a slight and gradual change under a democratic system. Because all points on the political spectrum are relative, those on the right consider moderates leftists, and those on the left consider them rightists.

For obvious reasons, in El Salvador (and most other developing countries) the poor tend to be leftists, the rich tend to be rightists, and the middle class holds a more moderate position for change without warfare. There are, of course, many exceptions to this general rule.

Feudalism versus Freedom • Salvadoran politics, like politics anywhere else, is neither simple nor clear-cut. To say that those on the right are capitalists and those on the left are communists would be an error of generalization and oversimplification.

The rightists are not fighting for capitalism as much as for the preservation of the social, political, and economic system that has prevailed over the last century. In this system, a member of the lower class, no matter how intelligent or hardworking, has no opportunity to rise up from the poverty he or she was born into. A member of the upper class, on the other hand, need not demonstrate any exceptional skill or intelligence in order to stay rich or get richer. Not unlike one born into royalty, an individual born into the upper class is assured a good life.

Although most land and businesses are privately owned, the oligarchic system in El Salvador is considered more feudalistic than capitalistic. The majority of the population earns only enough to survive until the next harvest. Because of their lower-class status, they will never own any private property except, at best, a small plot of land, which they are likely to lose all too soon. The capitalistic concept of success through ability and hard work does not apply to the lower class.

The picture of El Salvador as a feudalistic state is completed by the relationship of the armed forces, the upper class, and the government. The military officers are under the financial influence of the upper class. Nationally, the upper class has determined who is elected to office. Locally, the landowners of a given area can dictate the actions of the military in that area. If a landowner needs the local National Guard to break up a labor strike on his farm, soldiers will be sent. If a particular individual is talking too much about higher wages or constitutional justice, a landowner can have him arrested without criminal charges or trial. Although such things may be technically illegal, there is no one to enforce the laws that the armed forces are told to break. As a result, brute force tends to replace capitalism as the means for determining who is rich and who is poor.

Because the government and the upper class consider themselves capitalists, they call their opposition communists. In many cases, though by no means all, this accusation is accurate and fully warranted. Many of the guerrillas and leftist parties have accepted the beliefs of Karl Marx and have intentions of one day making El Salvador a communist country, following the model of Cuba or the Soviet Union.

As more and more people join the various guerrilla organizations and leftist political parties, an increasing majority know nothing about Karl Marx, communism, or the international politics involving the communist powers. They are fighting the government simply because they want change. Some of the changes are somewhat Marxist in nature, such as the redistribution of land. But even then, most people want the distributed land to be private property, not farms owned by the state, as they are in communist countries.

Hard-line Marxists want the state to own all businesses and industries. More moderate leftists think the state should control only key industries, such as banks and agricultural companies. Many so-called leftists, perhaps the majority, have no opinion about degrees of socialism. They only want to bring down the government that has been using military force to prevent any form of social, economic, or political improvement in the status of the lower class.

The Roots of the Conflict • In the 1500s and 1600s, when the first settlers were arriving in the Americas, the Industrial Revolution had already begun in England. With factories supplying not only products but jobs as well, ownership of land became less important. Through hard work, self-development, and the spirit of capitalism, it was possible for a hard worker to move up in the world. A middle class developed. Poverty was not necessarily permanent.

At the same time, democracy was beginning to develop in England. Religious freedom, though not perfect, was certainly better than in Spain, where the Spanish Inquisition was using force to eliminate any threat to the power of the Catholic Church. Neither religious tolerance nor democracy was developing.

When the first English settlers came to North America, they brought with them a respect for freedom and tolerance. They also brought a work ethic that encouraged personal growth through hard work, long-term invest-ment, and good ideas. They believed that a social and political system could be changed for the better.

It is also significant that these settlers came to the New World with the intention of staying. This meant they would have to build a lasting society that would see to the needs of their descendants.

Meanwhile, Spain and Portugal were barely emerg-ing from the Dark Ages. Feudalism was still strong, and industry was virtually nonexistent. There was no middle class, no way to rise above poverty. The national wealth came not from production but rather from gold. The New World was seen as a source of gold, not as a place to develop. The settlers came to conquer Indians and sail away with their gold, not to farm land and build cities. The leaders were aristocrats and their followers were serfs.

These early explorers of Latin America brought their feudalistic traditions with them. While the English settlers were building small, family farms in North America, the Spanish conquistadors in Central America were grabbing up vast tracts of land that they would never be able to develop, land they probably wouldn't even live on. They created their own fiefdoms in the New World.

North America, of course, was not entirely free of an economy that depended on cheap peasant labor on huge plantations. The American South, before the Civil War, was very similar to the Latin American economy in that it depended on slave labor. But the Civil War ended that.

So while democracy bloomed and flourished in North America, South and Central America remained under the control of a small wealthy class—direct descen-dants of the first aristocratic explorers—and strong, dic-tatorial governments. Since the wealth lay in the hands of those who had political power, social and economic changes were slow to come. In fact, in many ways, only today are some parts of the region beginning to change.

Unfortunately, the change seems possible only through violence. Where there is no democratic process, there is no way to change gradually and peacefully. Until recently, Latin America had no stable democratic governments. Just as the United States needed a civil war to end an economy based on cheap labor by a lower class, Latin America is now fighting several civil wars at various levels of conflict that might have similar outcomes. El Salvador is involved in one of these conflicts.

The Beginnings of Division • Liberals and conservatives have been at odds since the beginning of Salvadoran history in 1821, when the country gained independence from Spain. At that time, the conservatives were those who wanted to retain the social and political system the Spanish had created. The liberals wanted to change to a less feudalistic system.

During the first half of the nineteenth century, the chief crop was indigo, which was used to make a blue dye. The farmers were Indians living and working on communal plantations. As the years went by, many of these Indians adopted the Spanish language and way of life. In this period, the upper class were those of Spanish descent whose parents had been given large parcels of land by the Spanish government.

Coffee was introduced around 1850, at about the time that Germany developed a synthetic blue dye. Fortunately, as the need for indigo fell, the worldwide demand for coffee rose.

To hasten the agrarian transformation to an economy based on coffee, the government banned communal plantations and offered possession of the land to anyone who planted coffee on it. Although this made it easier for poor Indians to own their own land, it also made it easier for wealthier people to buy the small plots that had once been communal property but were now owned and readily sold by individual Indians.

Because coffee needs more care than indigo, the large plantations needed many workers. To help provide this labor, the government passed a law prohibiting persons from not working. A special police force was in charge of rounding up loitering Indians and putting them to work on coffee plantations. This force also broke up protests and arrested those who spoke out against the law.

This was the beginning of a hundred-year history of government control of the lower class for the benefit of the upper class, a continuation of the essentially feudalistic system Spain had imposed on all of Latin America. By the end of the nineteenth century, the infamous "Fourteen Families," who owned most of the coffee land and controlled the banks and export companies, were the "royalty" of El Salvador. Today the lower class still refers to the upper class as the "Fourteen Families," although they now number some three hundred families.

Coffee proved so profitable that it did not pay to use land to grow food. Salvadorans, especially those who owned the coffee land, found it wiser to export coffee and use the income to import food from other countries.

Though Salvadoran society had divided into upper and lower classes, the concept of leftist and rightist did not emerge until shortly after 1929, the beginning of the Great Depression.

Depression and Revolution • The Great Depression crippled the economy of the entire world. Companies went bankrupt, workers lost their jobs, and many people did not have money for basic foods, let alone the luxury of coffee.

El Salvador, dependent on the sale of coffee in the international market, with little land available for growing food crops, was hard hit. No one had enough money to buy Salvadoran coffee, and the country had no land on which to grow food.

The Salvadoran poverty of the 1930s was even worse than that of today. As coffee exports fell from $16 million in 1928 to only $4.8 million in 1932, daily wages on the plantations fell from 50 cents to 20 cents. As subsistence farmers sold their land for money to pay debts, the poverty spread.

Mao Zedong, a leader of the communist revolution in China, once wrote that poverty is the sea where communist fish swim best. During the depression of 1932, El Salvador became a classic example of communism thriving in poverty. As the Salvadorans had nothing to lose, they were quite willing to try anything new.

In 1930, Agustín Farabundo Martí, who had helped organize the Central American Socialist party, founded the Salvadoran Communist party. He believed that a lower-class revolution would bring about economic equality and social justice under a communist system of government.

Martí had experience with revolutions. He had worked with Agusto César Sandino, who was leading a guerrilla war against the Nicaraguan government and the U.S. Marines who had occupied Nicaragua in an attempt to stop communism in Central America. Sandino, who was actually fighting against U.S. intervention rather than in favor of communism, later became the namesake of the Sandinista revolutionaries who in 1979 overthrew the rightist dictatorship of Anastasio Somoza. Likewise, Farabundo Martí's name would later be used by a Salvadoran guerrilla organization, the Farabundo Martí National Liberation Front, or FMLN, its Spanish acronym.

The poor people of El Salvador knew nothing about communism, but they liked the sound of its slogans: Power to the People, Land for Everyone, Justice and Equality, and others that promised to make the dreams of the landless come true.

But the peasants who were supposed to fight the army were by no means soldiers. They were farmers—mostly poor Indians—from the countryside. Disorganized and without adequate weapons, they were no match for the army. The rebels killed fewer than seventy people before the army resumed total control.

The army proceeded to kill anyone who even looked like an Indian. Within a matter of weeks, they slaughtered between 15,000 and 30,000 people. The exact death toll is not known because all government records from that time have disappeared. Rightists now claim the lower number, leftists claim the higher, and the truth probably lies somewhere in between.

The unsuccessful rebellion of 1932 resulted in the virtual extinction of the Salvadoran Indian culture and the assumption of total power by the rightists—the military and the upper class. Since then, the upper class has controlled the military and the military has controlled the government.

Fifty Years of Military Rule • Few national elections in the half century since 1932 have been free of accusations of cheating by the government. An army officer always won and called himself "presidente," just as most Latin American dictators do.

There have been a few quick and bloodless coups, too, in which a group of officers joined forces, threw out the old dictator, declared a democracy, and installed a new dictator as president. The upper class often instigated these coups. When they felt that the old government was be-

The business district of
San Salvador in 1931

ginning to "lean to the left" by tolerating labor unions or allowing the Communist party to participate in an election, they simply hired a group of officers to follow their orders.

The Salvadoran government controls the country with the army, the National Guard, and the national police force. The army is in charge of protecting the country from foreign invasion. A recent major job has been the prevention of arms smuggling into El Salvador from Nicaragua.

The National Guard controls the general population by preventing general uprisings and fighting guerrillas. The National Guard bases in each area of the country operate more or less independently, with local commanders controlling a territory they consider their own domain.

The national police force is in charge of keeping order in towns. With very little direction from the central government, the police as well as the National Guard often serve as private armies for local landowners. They can be called upon to chase away squatters or "take care of" union leaders, leftists, and other "subversives" suspected of trying to stir up trouble.

The armed forces are supported by the Customs Police, who counter smuggling, and the Treasury Police, who help keep order on the cash-crop plantations and are feared for their use of torture.

By 1967 the government began to worry about the rise in leftist activity. Secret unions were being formed, workers were whispering about strikes, a few priests were beginning to use the pulpit to call for social justice, and university students were holding secret meetings to discuss Marxism. To keep an eye on these and other activities, the Ministry of Defense had created a special paramilitary organization called ORDEN, which means "order" in Spanish and represents a translation of National Democratic Organization.

ORDEN was a national network of civilians who, hoping for jobs in the government or monetary rewards, turned in information to the ministry about subversion—a report on a priest whose sermon raised questions about the un-Christian behavior of the government, news about a secret labor union planning a strike, or observations of people offering support, anything from food to weapons, to guerrillas.

Although the identities of the ORDEN network of local spies were to be kept secret, the people they spied on gradually figured out who they were. The civilians killed by guerrillas, a rare occurrence, were usually members of ORDEN.

The establishment of ORDEN marked an escalation in the conflict between the military government and those who wanted to bring change to Salvadoran society. As violence increased on both sides, the prospects of finding a peaceful solution to El Salvador's problems grew dimmer.

3

In 1972 the mayor of San Salvador, José Napoleón Duarte, decided to run for president. The son of a tailor and a simple peasant woman, Duarte was very popular among the people. He had been educated in the United States, at Notre Dame, one of the few Salvadorans who had a higher education without the benefits of an upper-class background. As a college-educated civil engineer, Duarte's early career put him in the middle class.

His political career began in 1960 when he and some friends pondered whether a communist revolution was the only alternative to the rightist military government. Agreeing that the government was not good but that communist rule would be little better, the group founded the politically moderate Christian Democratic party (Partido Demócrata Cristiano, PDC). This party became popular overnight. Today it may be the best alternative to the military government.

In 1964 Duarte became mayor of San Salvador, the highest position a civilian could realistically hope to hold.

Reelected twice, he was encouraged to run for president in 1972. Because Duarte seemed to have the best chance of winning, the other civilian candidates decided to support him and his running mate, Guillermo Ungo, in their campaign against the military government.

On the night of the election, the military was shocked to see the impossible happening. Duarte and Ungo were winning! Never before had anyone come close to defeating the military candidate backed by the upper class. Suddenly the radio stations stopped reporting the election results. Soldiers burst into the polling places and seized the ballot boxes.

The next morning the news reported that the military had been reelected and communism defeated by the majority of Salvadoran voters. Meanwhile, Duarte was arrested, tortured so badly that he lost two fingers, and put on a plane to Venezuela. He would not return for eight years.

The government immediately clamped down on all political activity. All nonrightist political parties were declared illegal. The university was shut down. Union organizers and peasant leaders were arrested or even shot on sight. ORDEN was given permission to help police and the National Guard to round up anyone who might cause trouble. Many of the sudden assassinations in the streets were carried out by unofficial ORDEN death squads so that no one could complain about police brutality.

The repression did not squelch completely all opposition to the government. In 1975, a church-sponsored peasant organization and countrywide farm workers' union joined forces to form the People's Revolutionary Bloc (BPR), which represented more than 100,000 people. They protested the repression with massive street demonstrations and labor strikes against farms and factories. Although their actions often led to bloodshed when the armed forces moved in, they at least managed to show the government that a great number of people were displeased with the situation, and that if things did not improve, there might someday be considerable support for the more militant guerrillas.

The Guerrillas • Guerrilla bands began to form in the early 1970s as peasants began to feel frustration at their hopeless situation and anger at the government that was using force to repress the lower class. The guerrillas, both men and women, were mostly in their twenties and thirties, though some were under fourteen or over sixty-five. They wore no uniforms except perhaps a certain-color beret or neckerchief. They received no pay and often had to find their own food and arms. To prevent the revealing of identities under torture, they called each other by code names.

They began as separate guerrilla groups, such as the People's Liberation Army, the Armed Forces of National Resistance, and eventually, in 1980, the Armed Forces of Liberation (an armed branch of the Salvadoran Communist party). Each had its own political ideology, ranging from strict Marxist communism to moderate socialism to merely antigovernment liberation.

In October 1980 the various groups united to form the Farabundo Martí National Liberation Front (FMLN). The FMLN says it intends to establish a democracy and to allow some private enterprise and that it does not intend to become a close ally of either the United States or the Soviet Union. Its ranks include university professors, ex-government officials, army deserters, doctors, and priests, although most members are *campesinos*. The total number of armed guerrillas is now estimated at 5,000 to 8,000.

Not listed as "official" guerrillas are the uncountable thousands of peasants who supply food and shelter to guerrillas and refuse to cooperate with the armed forces in their search for guerrillas. Because it is impossible to

Wearing uniforms stolen during an attack,
these FMLN guerrillas are taking their five
prisoners to a place where they were released
to the International Red Cross.

determine who is a sympathizer or even who is an actual guerrilla, the armed forces frequently kill innocent people. With each death, the number of guerrilla sympathizers grows.

During the 1980s, guerrilla support increased in the countryside and the army became less capable of strong incursions far from San Salvador. Thus the guerrillas were able to establish "liberated" areas. Here the Salvadoran government has no presence or power. The guerrillas and leftist sympathizers oversee production on cooperative farms, collect taxes, maintain a police force and judicial system, and operate schools and hospitals. For many peasants, this is the first time they have had access to such things as legal justice, medical attention, and police protection.

But guerrilla justice is, in some ways, similar to the military's idea of justice. Just as the military executes a suspected guerrilla sympathizer, the guerrillas have killed the mayors of several small towns in order to eliminate government presence there. The murders also intimidate government officials elsewhere.

Most of these liberated zones are in the interior and northern sections of the country. About one third of the area of the country and about 250,000 people are under guerrilla control.

The extent of democracy in these areas is questionable. Families that do not support the guerrilla movement with "voluntary" labor may be forced to move out. Anyone who helps the government military forces may be killed. Young men are under extreme pressure to join the guerrillas or to leave the liberated zone. Everyone is expected to attend guerrilla-led "consciousness-raising" meetings that non-sympathizers would probably call communist propaganda or even mild brainwashing.

The liberated zones are permanent and secure

enough to allow the FMLN to fabricate surprisingly sophisticated weaponry. Land mines have been their most effective weapon. They have been effective in two ways. They cause most of the casualties in the military forces, and they make soldiers afraid to venture into new territory or even off a secure road or path. Unfortunately, many of the casualties have been children who have wandered away from their yards.

Most guerrilla weapons and ammunition are captured from the army. It is probably true but unproven that some weapons come from Nicaragua and Cuba.

Though by no means as brutal as the army, the guerrillas do not tolerate opposition in the areas they control. Some informants and government sympathizers are killed, but more often they are simply forced to leave the area. Torture, which is still widely used by the military, is rarely, if ever, committed by the guerrillas.

To the army, everyone within a liberated area is probably a guerrilla or a guerrilla sympathizer. When planes drop bombs or helicopters strafe a suspected guerrilla stronghold, they are not usually concerned with the difference between civilian and guerrilla. Consequently, many areas prefer to remain "unliberated." The ideal situation seems to be when both the army and the guerrillas are trying to win the support of a local population. Often the army is there during the day, but the soldiers leave before nightfall, when the guerrillas are most active.

Talk of Land Reform • After four years of unrest and increased guerrilla activity following the 1972 elections, the government concluded that repression was not the answer. In 1976 the military offered a land-reform plan to the lower class in return for their support.

The land-reform plan, designed to redistribute the large plantations among the poor, limited the size of private landholdings to a maximum of 40 hectares (100 acres)—considerably less than the thousands of hectares owned by many. To test the plan, the government said it would first try out the plan in a limited area. If everyone cooperated, that is, if the guerrillas ceased their operations, the plan would include the whole country.

Having never known their government to be honest, the peasants suspected that this limited plan was just a trick to persuade them to stop supporting the leftists. The rich, on the other hand, were afraid that the government might actually go through with the plan, thus ending their wealth.

Consequently, no one was happy. The land-reform plan was never carried out, leftist discontent was as strong as ever, and in 1977 another fraudulent election brought a new military man to power, General Carlos Humberto Romero.

Repression Intensified • General Romero, defense minister under the preceding president, had helped to create ORDEN. He was put in office to stop the leftists once and for all, and he went to work with an iron fist. When a large but peaceful crowd of demonstrators filled the downtown streets of San Salvador to protest Romero's illegal election, National Guard soldiers killed more than a hundred people.

Romero instituted a state of emergency, which allowed him and the armed forces to bypass many laws. Police began arresting students who dared to discuss Marxist philosophy, priests who called for social justice, teachers who taught the meaning of democracy in class, peasants who were away from their hometowns without good reason, and anyone who was even slightly suspected of being antigovernment or pro-guerrilla.

In towns all over the country, jeeps and army trucks

were heard after the 11 P.M. curfew as the soldiers rounded up "subversives." From outside of town, gunshots were heard. In the morning, peasants found dead friends and neighbors along the roads or in parking lots. The bodies often showed signs of torture. Anyone daring to complain to the police was arrested, beaten, or killed by a death squad.

The seriousness of the Salvadoran situation gained worldwide attention when twenty-two unarmed protesters were machine-gunned on the steps of a San Salvador cathedral. News cameras caught the action, and the next day the massacre was seen all over the world.

The forces on the right had reason for their nervous trigger fingers. The left was becoming just as desperately violent as the right. The guerrillas, ranging from hard-line communists to apolitical people who simply wanted to fight the government, started a strategy of destabilization. In an effort to make the government seem unstable and weak, they raided power plants, government vehicles and buildings, factories and farms. Every time they caused a blackout or tied up traffic, they made the government seem incapable of running the country. Such actions provoked violent military reaction, which made the government seem even more cruel and persuaded more people to rise up in revolt.

In a rolling snowball effect, the violence increased. A guerrilla could be anybody, a ten-year-old boy or an eighty-year-old woman. Soldiers, not knowing who was friend or foe, killed many innocent people through sheer fear and nervousness. The needless killings only made more enemies, which in turn increased the soldiers' over-reactions.

Not all the killings were accidents or the result of self-defense. The rightists often frightened the *campesinos* into submission. Rather than simply leave a dead body beside the road, they might cut off parts of the body or leave obvious signs of beating or burning, thus suggesting that there were things worse than death to fear. But the fact that peasants dared to strike back indicated that they feared something even more than death and torture—the continuation of poverty and repression.

The Role of the Church • In the midst of the violence in 1977, the Catholic Church, to which 80 percent of the Salvadoran population belongs, began to take an active role in the country's politics.

For more than 350 years, the Catholic Church in El Salvador and the other Latin American countries taught the poor that their suffering would ensure their eventual entrance into heaven, that misery is a part of life, and that God has reasons for creating certain conditions here on earth. These teachings accounted for much of the lower class's acceptance of its fate.

In 1977, however, two events caused the Church to veer onto a new course: Oscar Arnulfo Romero (no relation to General Romero) became archbishop of El Salvador, and his good friend Father Rutilio Grande was machine-gunned to death by hired assassins.

Rutilio Grande, a Jesuit priest, believed in the "Theology of Liberation," an idea inspired by the 1968 Latin American Bishops' Conference in Medellin, Colombia. There Pope Paul said that the Church should take a more active role in the care of the poor. Although he did not mean that priests should take a political stance, many felt that in Latin America, defending the poor was in itself a political position. Rutilio Grande's outspoken defense of the poor and his criticism of the government were interpreted by some as a call for communist revolution. Someone, perhaps the government itself, thought this justified his assassination.

Rutilio Grande's death caused a radical shift in

the previously conservative Archbishop Romero. After that, Romero felt he could no longer turn his back on the brutality of his government and the injustices of social and economic division in his country. His sermons began to relate the scriptures of the Bible to the plight of the peasants. He told them that God did not want them to live in misery, that simply because they were human they had a right to fill their stomachs and farm their own land and sleep without fear of soldiers invading their homes.

To help the poor comfort each other, the Church organized discussion groups that met in private homes to talk about religion and its relation to their lives. These meetings brought about a new awareness among the people of the lower class; and for this reason, the government considered them a form of subversion meant to stir up revolutionary trouble. People caught attending the meetings were often arrested and never seen again.

In response, the Church established a Legal Aid Society to keep a record of deaths, arrests, disappearances, beatings, and incidents of torture. Legal Aid also tried to obtain the release of people from prison before they "disappeared" from all records. Although individual peasants could not dare to complain openly about such things, the Church had enough power and anonymity to protest out loud. Today, its records are considered more honest and accurate than those of the government.

Increase in Guerrilla Activity • During 1978 and 1979 several independent guerrilla organizations were formed to perform specific tasks. The Popular Revolutionary Bloc could, on a moment's notice, rally tens of thousands of people for street protests or the peaceful takeover of a government building or foreign embassy. The Popular Revolutionary Army excelled at bombing government buildings, cars, and homes. The Armed Forces of National Resistance became experts at kidnapping important businessmen, government officials, and foreigners.

Kidnapping was an especially effective leftist tactic—high ransoms allowed the purchase of more weapons. The ransom publicity has also helped focus worldwide attention on their power and the grievances they have against the government. For example, when two American businessmen were kidnapped, part of the ransom demand was that their company pay for political advertisements in U.S. newspapers.

The two U.S. businessmen and a Peace Corps volunteer who was kidnapped later were all released unharmed, but others were not as fortunate. Many were killed after the guerrillas collected the ransom. The overall effect has served to further destabilize the country as many upper-class businessmen, bankers, landowners, and other educated people essential to the economic system flee to Miami. At the same time, no foreign businessmen and few tourists come to El Salvador, and foreign investors are pulling out of the country.

By 1979 the violence was spiraling upward as each side had increasingly good reasons to fear and hate the other. With every atrocity committed by one side, the other would react with even greater vengeance. As El Salvador moved toward all-out civil war, the U.S. government tried to help President Romero find a solution.

The violence in El Salvador seemed to be following the pattern developing in neighboring Nicaragua. The rightist dictator, Anastasio Somoza, who had always used repression to defend the Nicaraguan oligarchy, was battling an uprising of almost everyone from the lower and middle classes. He had never used free elections or talk of land reform to pacify the leftists, and now, in 1978 and 1979, though his army was gradually deserting him, he was sure he could win a military victory over the guerrillas.

Residents of a town attacked by leftist guerrillas stare at the smoldering ruins of the town's civil defense garrison and town hall.

Meanwhile, President Jimmy Carter requested that the U.S. ambassador to El Salvador, Frank Devine, meet often with President Romero in an attempt to work out a peaceful solution to the country's problem. The United States did not want El Salvador to become another Nicaragua, and it was felt that free elections would be a big step toward peace.

Romero doubted that free elections would be honest. He almost admitted that the rightists had illegally influenced elections in the past and that leftists had tried to do the same. It was unlikely that they would not try again in the future. He and other government officials also expressed fear that the United States was trying to impose a Christian Democratic government on El Salvador, as that party would probably win a free election, as it had in 1972. Ambassador Devine also met with leftist leaders, who maintained that free elections were impossible because the rightists would harass or even assassinate candidates.

But in August 1979 President Romero promised free elections in 1980 with neutral foreign officials present at the polls and the complete cooperation of the armed forces. This promise never became action, however, and the repression continued as before. It seemed that President Romero intended to follow Nicaraguan president Somoza's strategy—guns, not ballots, would defeat the guerrillas.

Rumors of a Coup • Ambassador Devine said later that he had heard rumors of another coup coming up in El Salvador, but he could not determine its origin. The extreme right might try in an effort to stop elections. The more moderate right might try in an attempt to stop the repression and make elections possible.

In October, two army colonels walked into President Romero's office and informed him that he was no longer president. Romero made a few phone calls to other officers and to the U.S. embassy, discovered that no one was supporting him, and promptly fled to Guatemala, taking his loyal generals with him.

The young officers who were now in charge declared a state of emergency and announced a plan to renew peace in El Salvador. The new government would be a *junta*—a group of men who would lead the government, rather than just one. Some of the members of the junta would be civilians, others would be military leaders. The left and the right would be equally represented. Together (junta means "together" in Spanish) they would stop the fighting by curing its causes, not by attacking its symptoms.

As the officers hastily pulled together a workable junta, the leftists held fire and the people held their collective breath. This junta seemed to be their last chance for peace.

Many people feel that the United States indirectly encouraged this coup by expressing support of any democratic government that tries to help its citizens. Perhaps this is the reason the young officers suggested a civilian-military junta as a prelude to elections and true democracy. Maybe they wanted peace and democracy, or maybe they simply hoped to put on an appearance of progress toward those ends.

The junta did not work well. The more liberal members dropped out and were replaced by more conservative and militaristic individuals. Military repression continued. Democracy seemed no closer than before, until the United States decided to influence the situation.

4

PROGRESS TOWARD DEMOCRACY

Colonel Jáime Gutiérrez and Colonel Adolfo Arnoldo Majano, the young officers who ousted President Romero in 1979, had an interesting and innovative plan for neutralizing the leftists. By promising to give the country what the leftists were demanding, the colonels hoped to encourage people to support the government instead of the guerrillas. The promises were land reform and an end to governmental and military repression.

If the new government could accomplish these changes, the guerrillas would have no reason to fight. If they continued their rebellion despite the changes, it would prove that power, not social reform, was their goal. The peasant masses that had been supporting the guerrillas would choose to support the government that was, at last, helping them.

The colonels had good reason to fear increasing guerrilla activity. Three months earlier, the oligarchic and rightist government of Nicaragua, led by Anastásio So-

Col. Jaime Gutierrez (left) and Col. Adolfo Majano,
the officers who ousted President Carlos Romero
in 1979, hold their first news conference.
They believed that if they gave the Salvadorans
needed land reform and stopped repression that
the people would no longer support the guerrillas.
But this did not happen.

moza, had fallen to leftist Sandinista guerrillas. The question now was whether El Salvador's future would parallel that of Nicaragua's past: a leftist victory after a fight to the finish against the government.

The United States was also concerned. Though President Carter was not disappointed to see the cruel and corrupt Somoza government fall, he was not pleased with the leftist Sandinista government either. After a little initial economic support, the Congress and the president noticed that Nicaragua was accepting a lot of military aid from the Soviet Union and Cuba. U.S. support promptly came to an end, and Nicaragua fell into the Soviet sphere of influence. It looked like "another Cuba," but this time on the mainland and right next door to El Salvador.

To encourage El Salvador to carry out social reforms, the United States insisted on civilian participation in the government and an end to death squad activities.

The junta took on some civilian members, including Guillermo Ungo, the vice-presidential candidate who had been ousted after the 1972 election. But the awkward combination of leaders made little progress. When the colonels and Defense Minister José Garcia met with human-rights groups to show their new concern for justice, they were unwilling or unable to answer questions about hundreds of missing people and death squad victims. A few weeks later, when soldiers machine-gunned a crowd of demonstrators, killing twenty-four, Defense Minister Garcia refused to allow an investigation. He made it obvious that the military was still running the country.

By January 1980 the junta broke up. The civilian members refused to participate. One cabinet member, Rubén Zamora, fled the country after his brother, Manò, El Salvador's attorney general, was murdered in his home. Three other cabinet ministers also joined leftist guerrilla groups. Guillermo Ungo fled the country and eventually became head of the Democratic Revolutionary Front (Frente Democratico Revolucionário, or FDR), a non-military political union of several parties opposing the government.

A second civilian-military junta fared no better. There was no progress toward land reform and no end to government repression. Archbishop Oscar Romero, asking his Catholic flock to give the junta a chance, warned that "the time for legitimate violence [against the government] was fast approaching." These were radical words for such a high member of the Church hierarchy. He was not advocating a Marxist government, though. His philosophy criticized the fallacies of both capitalism and communism.

But the archbishop went too far when he urged soldiers to obey the law of God that says, "Thou shalt not kill" and to disobey the less authoritative orders of their officers. The government could not tolerate such words. "An army that does not kill is not much of an army," they said. The government charged the archbishop with inciting soldiers to mutiny.

The next day, as he was saying mass at a hospital chapel, an assassin's bullet struck his heart. Though the last word to leave his lips was "justice," his killer would never be found.

A few days later, at a demonstration protesting the lack of government reaction to the murder, a crowd of 100,000 was first sprayed with poison by a crop duster and then machine-gunned by an army unit. Twenty-one people died.

Again, the civilians of the junta resigned. The United States, recognizing that the military still held absolute power, threatened to withdraw all military and economic support. Desperate for a better image, the junta convinced

José Napoleón Duarte to join them. They also took control of all the banks in the country and enacted a Land Reform Act.

It was an uncomfortable situation. Duarte was supposed to control the military that had ignored his election in 1972 and then imprisoned and tortured him. Now the military had to tolerate him or face the loss of U.S. support. In 1980 and early 1981, U.S. military aid would reach $10.7 million.

Not surprisingly, political progress was slow. Duarte had little support in the government. The guerrillas, hoping to overthrow the government before it moved toward social reform and before the U.S. elections, launched their "final offensive."

But the offensive failed. It was very significant that the general population did not rally to fight the government, as had happened in Nicaragua. The guerrillas fled to the jungles and mountains, wounded but not defeated.

The junta hobbled on. Death squad murders increased. In December 1980, three nuns and a woman church worker were raped and murdered by members of an army unit. In a trial that captured headlines around the world, the military managed to lay the blame on a few young recruits. No officers were implicated, though certainly the boys had been ordered to do what they confessed to have done. But it satisfied the requirements of the U.S. government. Economic and military aid continued.

A Series of Successful Elections • In 1982, El Salvador held elections for a Constituent Assembly that would resemble the U.S. House of Representatives. Observers from several countries verified that the votes were cast and counted honestly. But that didn't necessarily mean the elections were completely honest. According to the guerrillas and most leftist parties, they could not campaign in public because death squads were still killing anyone who

José Napoléon Duarte at a 1982 press conference.
In 1985 he became president.

spoke against the military or upper class. They therefore refused to run for office.

Under such conditions, it was no surprise that the biggest victor in the elections was a coalition of rightist parties called ARENA. Its leader was Roberto D'Aubuisson, who had been connected with death squad killings and is widely believed to have been involved in the murder of Archbishop Romero. Supported by landowners and business people and even some of the peasant class, he and the ARENA coalition would be an obstacle to any type of social reform, especially land reform.

In 1985, national elections made José Napoleón Duarte president of El Salvador. Again he had to struggle to make progress. The National Assembly was controlled by the rightists. The leftists did not believe Duarte would be able to do much. But he did manage to abolish the Treasury Police and ORDEN, both of which had been linked to death squad activities. (ORDEN stands for Organización Democrática Nacionalista. It was a civilian paramilitary network of 50,000 to 100,000 people, founded in 1968.) He also opened negotiations with the guerrillas. Consequently, his moderate Christian Democratic Party (PDC) won more seats than ARENA in the new legislative and municipal elections of 1985.

But the Christian Democratic party soon became mired in corruption. When an earthquake hit San Salvador in 1986, foreign governments and international relief organizations sent millions of dollars in aid to El Salvador. But as the poor were quick to notice, not much reconstruction was carried out, though government officials were managing to build million-dollar mansions with salaries of under $30,000 a year. One candidate in the Christian Democratic party, a friend of Duarte's son, was accused of pocketing $2 million from a rural development program.

Inflation increased under the Duarte government. The price of beans, which arc found on the dinner table of anyone wealthy enough to afford a meal, tripled during the first two years of his administration. Soon the large, unwieldy one-colón coins became known as "Duartes" because they were virtually worthless and weren't worth the trouble of carrying around. To no one's surprise, the 1988 elections gave the ARENA party a majority of the sixty seats in the National Assembly and most of the mayoralties in 262 cities across the country.

President Duarte did manage to carry out part of the long-promised land reform. Some 26 percent of the rural population was either given land or allowed to participate in a cooperative farm. But the program was by no means a complete success. Many of the cooperatives went bankrupt due to lack of financial support.

Duarte's efforts and U.S. encouragement apparently had some effect. The 1980s saw five relatively honest elections in El Salvador, a virtual miracle for a country that had never had a single honest election. Political killings fell from 5,331 in 1982 to under 300 in 1985 and fewer than 20 in 1987. However, the numbers were rising again in 1988. Though the number of guerrillas remained more or less constant, the lower class was not rising en masse to support them.

In the late 1980s, the Salvadoran government estimated that between fifty and eighty thousand peasants, or about 1 percent of the population, supported the guerrillas with food, shelter, and information. Most other people, though, seemed to support whoever controlled their town at the time. They had seen local rightists killed by guerrillas and local leftists killed by the military, and many innocent people killed by the land mines and stray bullets of both sides. Most Salvadorans would just like to see an end to the war, no matter which side wins.

A Shift to the Right • The results of the national elections held in 1989 surprised many Americans, especially those in Washington, D.C. The rightist ARENA party won by a landslide, taking the presidency, a majority in the National Assembly, and most mayoralties. Duarte's Christian Democratic party ran a poor second, and Guillermo Ungo's coalition of moderately leftist parties won only 2 percent of the vote. The results were certainly affected by the corruption in the Duarte government, the fact that a third of the country was under guerrilla control, and the unwillingness of many leftists to run for office. Only 60 percent of the adult population voted.

The question among lawmakers in Washington was whether this turn to the right would mean a reversal of the land reform, a revival of the death squads, and a return to fraudulent elections.

The newly elected president, Alfredo "Fredy" Cristiani, claimed that this was a new and moderate ARENA party. Its founder, Roberto D'Aubuisson, long associated with death squads, insisted that he was no longer in a position of power in the party.

The election did not go smoothly. The guerrilla forces did everything they could to disrupt the process. The sabotage of power and water lines left most of the country in the dark and without water. Highways were blocked and buses were threatened with destruction. Thirty-three people died in fighting, including three foreign journalists. Two of the journalists were apparently machine-gunned shortly after showing their identification papers at an army roadblock.

How would Washington react to all this after trying so hard to keep the moderate, centrist Christian Democrats in power? A report in the *New York Times* quoted Senator Christopher J. Dodd as saying, "Most members of Congress will be willing to give the ARENA party an

CRISTIANI
EL PRESIDENTE
QUE TODOS QUEREMOS

In the 1989 elections, rightist ARENA party
candidate Alfredo Cristiani became president.
The main attraction for voters during the
campaign, however, was the presence of
Roberto D'Aubuisson, the ARENA party
founder, long associated with death squads.
D'Aubuisson is in the center, with Cristiani
and his wife to the right.

opportunity to demonstrate what it is going to do with its power. If it begins to turn a blind eye and a deaf ear to the re-emergence of death squads and human rights abuses by the military, then as sure as I am sitting here, you can count on resolutions being introduced in Congress to restrict American aid."

Negotiations • During the early 1980s, it was questioned whether the United States should encourage negotiations with the guerrillas. The guerrillas were claiming that they were a legitimate government that was forced to hide in the mountains or stay out of the country. They have refused to participate in elections because they fear assassination if they campaign in public. Since they have not been involved in elections, they feel that El Salvador's democratic decisions, including the constitution that was approved in 1984, are not legitimate. Many of the guerrilla demands, therefore, are in conflict with the constitution and the results of elections.

The guerrillas have demanded that the military forces be completely reorganized. They want to install guerrillas as officers in the army in order to guarantee the behavior of the military. Naturally, the government has refused to allow its enemy to join its army.

They have also been demanding that members of the leftist political parties replace many elected officials. President Ronald Reagan repeatedly called this an attempt by the guerrillas to "shoot their way into the government," which would be, by definition, antidemocratic.

Negotiations in 1987 almost resulted in progress. President Duarte held talks with the FDR political party and the FMLN guerrillas. It was decided that two government-rebel commissions would be established to negotiate a cease-fire. They would also discuss the proposals of a peace agreement that had been signed by the five Central American presidents in Guatemala City a few months before. The commissions held one round of talks but suspended further discussion when Herbert Anaya, a human rights activist, was assassinated by a death squad.

Negotiations in early 1989, just before the presidential election in March, appeared to take a big step forward. For the first time, guerrillas offered to participate in the elections. The conditions they demanded, however, were readily dismissed by the government. They wanted an 80 percent reduction of military forces, and the prosecution of politicians and army officers accused of human rights abuses.

Guillermo Ungo, the former vice-presidential candidate who had fled the country after serving on a junta, admitted that the demands were mostly an attempt at public relations. It was a way of pointing out what the guerrillas were fighting against. At the time, he and former minister Rubén Zamora were in El Salvador to lead a new coalition of leftist parties and, they hoped, to participate in the March 1989 elections. It is significant that they were able to do so and survive.

Economic Problems • No country ravaged by war can maintain a normal economy. This is especially true in El Salvador because the main thrust of guerrilla tactics has been to destroy the economy of the country. It is estimated that guerrilla action has caused damage exceeding $2 billion. By encouraging strikes, sabotaging factories, blowing up dams and bridges, and downing power lines, the guerrillas hope to drive the country into deep poverty. When people become dissatisfied with the government's ability to provide job security, food, electricity, and so on, they will, theoretically, rise in revolt.

This strategy may be hurting the guerrillas, however, since it has contributed to the demise of the cooperative

Pedestrians pull themselves up by ropes at a
bridge blown up by leftist guerrillas.
Guerrilla activity has caused billions of
dollars' worth of damage throughout the country.

farms that the land reform created. A strike in a chemical factory could mean a shortage of fertilizer. An ambushed truck means there is no way to transport crops to market. A blown-up power plant means a disruption in farm work. To people who have already gained a piece of land, guerrilla activities like these are a threat to a good situation, not a promise of change.

To make matters worse, the government funds that might pay for schools, hospitals, and roads must pay for guns and ammunition.

El Salvador is also suffering from *decapitalization*, the sending of money to other countries where it is safer. Afraid that a communist takeover would mean the end of their bank accounts, the upper class has sent well over $2.5 billion to banks in the United States, Switzerland, the Bahamas, and other countries. This amount is equal to about two-thirds of the aid that the United States has sent to El Salvador.

The unstable situation has also brought an end to foreign investment. No company wants to risk its money in a country that might fall to communist control.

The country has also been plagued by strikes. Some are inspired by or are in sympathy with the guerrillas. Others are in response to unfair treatment by the government. A strike by 1,500 hydroelectric workers blacked out the country and shut off San Salvador's water supply for twenty-four hours. One week 900 doctors went on strike to protest the army's killing of patients who were in the hospital after being wounded by bullets at a street demonstration. During the same week, 700 Agrarian Transformation workers went on strike to protest lack of government cooperation in the land reform program, and all teachers and court workers went on strike to protest the death squad murders of their co-workers.

The result has been a tragic increase in suffering among the poor. Unemployment in San Salvador is estimated at between 35 and 50 percent. Only one in ten Salvadoran peasants has access to safe drinking water—three less than the number in 1985. This lack of clean water is probably the main cause of the soaring rate of infant mortality. According to the U.S. Agency for International Development (AID), 43 out of 1,000 children die before the age of five, though this is an improvement from the 51 out of 1,000 average in 1985.

The Agency for International Development reports that El Salvador's gross national product has risen slightly each year since 1984. The benefits, however, seem to have fallen more on the side of the upper class, which has been weathering the war rather well. They still manage to drive new cars and eat at the new Pizza Hut and McDonald's restaurants in downtown San Salvador. Their sons are not drafted into the army, their nightclubs and discos are thriving, their mansions are still safe, and their foreign bank accounts are still waiting for the day things get too bad in El Salvador.

The Military Today • During the 1980s, the armed forces of El Salvador were built up from a poorly equipped and poorly trained force of 11,000 to a well equipped and better trained force of 57,000. Most of the enlisted men are from the lower class; most of the officers are from the upper class. Promotions are normally made according to how long an individual has been in service, not how well he has served.

Until recently, there were no legal restraints on the activities of the military. Though no one has doubted that the army has participated in thousands of murders, only eight soldiers have been put on trial, six of whom were tried for killing Americans. No officer had ever been accused of a crime until early 1989. In March of that year, just two weeks before the presidential elections, two officers and seven soldiers were charged with massacring ten unarmed civilians in 1988. American ambassador William Walker called the indictment a breakthrough that showed how El Salvador had changed after a decade of democracy. Diplomats from other countries, however, expressed doubts that the officers would be convicted. At worse, the soldiers would pay the price of following orders.

For several years the United States had had fifty-five military advisers in El Salvador. They are strictly forbidden to participate in fighting or even go into areas where a battle might occur. Their role has been to teach the Salvadoran armed forces to counter a guerrilla insurrection. Their lessons include something more than battlefield tactics and the use of modern weapons.

One important lesson they are teaching the Salvadorans is something that Americans learned in Vietnam: no military force can defeat a guerrilla army without winning the support of the civilian population.

The Salvadorans have learned the lesson well, but by no means perfectly. Colonel René Emilio Ponce, chief of staff of the Armed Forces, is forcing the army to develop new tactics. As one of the few high officers who accompanies his troops into guerrilla-held territory, he says that the best way to hurt the guerrillas is not to kill them but to take away their civilian support. He cultivates civilian support by asking peasants about their problems and seeing what he can do to help them.

But not all army officers have that same philosophy. In February 1989 a delegation of Americans accused a U.S.-trained battalion of killing a Mexican doctor, four Salvadoran nurses, and five injured rebels in an attack on a guerrilla hospital. There was evidence of rape in the case of the murdered women.

In early 1989 the Human Rights Office of the Catholic Church reported that both guerrilla and army murders

of civilians were rising. The total was 261 in 1988, up from 156 the year before. Government forces killed twice as many people as the guerrillas, but both groups were killing more than before.

Refugees • All wars send thousands of refugees fleeing from the cross fire. El Salvador is no exception. Some flee rightist death squads, some flee guerrilla domination, some flee the ruins of their homes after an army or air force attack. Sometimes the army forces civilians to leave an area. Somewhere between a quarter and a third of the population of El Salvador has had to leave the land or area they called home.

Most refugees stay within El Salvador. The capital, by far the largest city in the country, seems the obvious place to go. That refuge, however, is in many ways as bad as the battlegrounds. With the economy at a standstill, there are virtually no jobs in the city. More than a million people live in horrendous poverty. Shacks of scrap wood and flattened tin cans sprawl over the hillsides around the city. Families often have barely enough room for everyone to lie side by side on the floor at night. Virtually no one has access to clean drinking water, let alone running water in the house. As is common under such circumstances, alcoholism, domestic violence, and crime rates are high.

A U.S. adviser instructs a Salvadoran air force cadet in the use of an M-16 rifle in 1983. Advisers had been in El Salvador since mid-1981 to give instruction in counter-insurgency tactics.

Left: *War means refugees, and this is as
true in El Salvador as anywhere.
This family is being taken to a refugee camp.
Some people leave El Salvador, others remain.*

Above: *As in all wars, children are the
most heartbreaking victims. This is an
overcrowded classroom that also functions as
a dining room in a refugee center. The future
of these children looks bleak.*

The United Nations estimates that by the end of 1988, 164,800 Salvadorans had fled to other Central American countries. Mexico received the largest portion, some 120,000. Most refugees in Mexico live in camps in the southern part of the country. Another 55,000 refugees, most from Guatemala, worsen the situation. Poverty-stricken Mexico doesn't have enough jobs for its own people, so refugees have little hope of settling into Mexican society.

A *New York Times* report on refugees in a Honduran camp painted a sad scene. Since much of the fighting in El Salvador occurs near the Honduran border, many thousands have sought asylum there. Most of them are forced to remain in four camps that are financed by international relief organizations. Most of the refugees there are women, children, and elderly people. Men and women of military age are still in El Salvador, fighting for either the army or the guerrillas.

United Nations officials oversee the camps, but they can't do much to keep the conflict out. The Honduran army surrounds the camps to keep refugees from moving to the capital, Tegucigalpa, and to keep Salvadoran guerrillas from seeking asylum there. Nevertheless, leftists wield considerable power within the camps, and often Honduran soldiers enter to look for guerrillas. In a few instances, civilians have died in sudden bursts of shooting.

Nicaragua and Costa Rica have each absorbed about 7,000 refugees. These two countries quickly issue working permits in hopes of avoiding the problems brought on by camps.

The United Nations has been encouraging refugees to return to El Salvador. There has been limited success. About 1,000 people a year have been deciding that life would be better there than in the camps. In some cases, the U.N. gives them a little money—about $50—when they

Many Salvadoran refugees have fled to nearby Honduras. However, they are being pressured by Honduran authorities to leave certain camps because of the strategic importance of the sites. The Salvadorans, though, do not wish to return to their country until the war ends.

get to the border. The number of refugees choosing to return seems to be increasing, but the problem of overcrowded camps is bound to continue until the conflict in El Salvador ends.

It is estimated that perhaps as many as a million Salvadorans have managed to enter the United States, most illegally. Los Angeles and Washington, D.C., are said to have more Salvadorans than San Salvador has. Few of these individuals have been granted political asylum, which would entitle them to immigration visas and work permits. Church organizations, recognizing the danger these refugees would face if they returned to their country, have been active in sheltering and counseling them. An underground railroad, similar to the one that helped fleeing slaves escape their owners before the U.S. Civil War, has helped uncounted thousands of Salvadorans reach Canada, where immigration laws are not as strict.

5

LAND REFORM

The civilian-military junta that took power in late 1979 had good reason to immediately offer an extensive land reform to the people of El Salvador. The history of the twentieth century has shown that virtually every peasant revolt has occurred in countries where 30 percent or more of the rural population consisted of landless peasants. Such a situation existed in Mexico in 1911, Russia in 1917, the rice-growing regions of China in 1941, Bolivia in 1952, Cuba in 1959, South Vietnam in 1961, Ethiopia in 1975, Iran in 1979, and Nicaragua in 1979. And it was clearly happening in El Salvador in 1980, where landless peasants amounted to 70 percent of the rural population.

The junta announced the Agrarian Reform Act on March 6, 1980. It would be composed of three phases. Phase I, taking effect immediately, expropriated all estates of 500 hectares (1,250 acres) or more. The government took immediate title to the land with the intention of eventually passing ownership to the peasants who worked the land.

Phase II, to take effect in the future, would take over and distribute the medium-sized farms of 100 to 500 hectares (250 to 1,250 acres). These are the most desirable farms because they yield the most profitable cash crop, coffee, as well as a great deal of cotton and sugar.

Phase III, called the "land to the tiller" phase, was intended to give small plots of land to anyone who was renting or sharecropping the land. Most of these plots were less than 10 hectares (25 acres).

An immediate nationalization of all Salvadoran banks and agricultural export companies was included in the Land Reform Act. The nationalization gave the government 51 percent of the stock in each company and bank. Of the remainder, 20 percent could be owned by the employees of the companies and the rest was available to the public, though no individual could own more than 2 percent. With a majority of the stock in its possession, the government could control the policies and decisions of these companies. The upper class could not strangle the new farm cooperatives by cutting off their credit or their access to international markets. The grip of the upper class was loosened at last.

Phase I • The large estates affected by Phase I were to stay intact as cooperative farms. The *colonos* who had been working on them were to receive private plots of up to 7 hectares (17 acres), but they would share the resources of the farm, such as tractors, water, tools, irrigation equipment, trucks, and some of the land.

The original owners of these vast haciendas would receive 25 percent of their land's value in cash and the other 75 percent in special bonds that could be used only to invest in Salvadoran industries. The cash would support them for a while, and the investment bonds would keep the money in El Salvador and promote the development of industry.

At the same time, the *campesinos* were not given the land outright. They were to pay back the government over a thirty-year period. Some farmers managed to pay back most or even all of the money in a few years, but the majority had serious trouble doing this.

Phase I affected 263 estates, comprising some 249,000 hectares (615,000 acres). This amounted to about 17 percent of all farmland and about 23 percent of all cropland. About 22 percent of all coffee land, 28 percent of all cotton land, and 50 percent of all sugarcane land was turned over to 70,000 peasant families. About 40 percent of those families did not own any land, and about 75 percent of the people were families of former migrant workers.

Phase II • Phase II, which was supposed to expropriate most medium-sized farms, was never put into effect. Since most coffee plantations fell into this category, it was politically impossible to accomplish this. There was too much money involved. The government was also worried that exports would decline too much if peasants failed to run the coffee plantations efficiently. The country as a whole would suffer if its primary source of income was not kept up.

Leftists said that Phase II was never brought about because Phase I had served well as a "life insurance policy" for the upper class. It had cost a bit, but it had guaranteed the continuation of their unbroken power. Phase II, the leftists said, was the final step that would have achieved a complete social and economic revolution in El Salvador.

Phase III • Phase III expropriated all tenanted and share-cropped land. Anyone who was planting and harvesting on someone else's land received title to that land. This phase

At the largest coffee farm in
El Salvador, farmers sift beans.

redistributed almost half of El Salvador's arable land. Some 210,000 families—close to a million people— became landowners.

While this was certainly an important part of the land reform, it was criticized by rightists as doing little to discourage the rebellion. It only benefited those who already had access to the land, people who were relatively well off in comparison with the truly landless *jornaleros*. The millions of homeless migrant workers who were not working on a large farm when Phase I took effect and were not sharecropping land when Phase III took effect were completely left out.

Leftists complained that Phase III only affected the worst of the land in El Salvador. It was land that big farmers didn't want to be bothered with, land so rocky or steep that only a peasant could farm it by planting a little corn here and there. Since the government bought the land from the owners, it was actually a good way to sell poor land that the rich didn't want and the poor couldn't afford to buy.

Problems • Land reforms have been tried in many countries. Few, if any, have worked well. Recent examples in Latin America include Peru and Brazil. It seems that there are inevitable political problems when a country redistributes such a fundamental form of wealth. Sometimes the government promises a reform in order to drum up support among the poor, but then fails to carry out its promise. Sometimes the landowners and upper class use violence to prevent the expropriation or the success of the expropriated farm.

In El Salvador, the success of the land reform is debatable. Leftists claim that it is just a token offering aimed at keeping people from supporting the revolution. They say that as soon as the guerrilla forces are inactive,

Farmers during a lunch break. The success of land reform in El Salvador is open to question. Some believe that as soon as the guerrillas are defeated, things will go back to the way they were: With all the land in the hands of the wealthy.

the reform will be reversed, because the real power is still in the hands of the oligarchy.

They also claim that the government has designed the reform to fail. By demanding that the cooperative farms pay back the former owners too quickly, they doom the farms to bankruptcy. Eventually, they say, the land will return to the upper class.

Considering the political and economic situation in El Salvador, it's surprising that the land reform took place at all. It's even more surprising that it affected so much land and that so many people benefited. Beyond doubt, it was the most extensive land redistribution in modern times.

There was considerable violence when the land reform first took effect. Landowners were understandably angry. In many cases, they stripped the farm of all equipment, even the fencing. Meanwhile, the civil war had been raging around the farms, making it hard to truck crops to the cities and ports. In many cases, former owners hired death squads to kill the leaders of the cooperative organizations.

The biggest barrier to success was the new landowners themselves. Overnight, they changed from serfs to partners in a big business. These peasants, who had never before had land or the responsibility of running a farming business, were completely incapable of efficient operations. Since few of them could read, they had no way of learning how to use fertilizer and insecticides, operate equipment, or keep good records. Never having had any money, they knew nothing about how supply and demand affect prices. Profit and investment were foreign concepts to them. In fact, the average peasant knew virtually nothing about the intricacies of farming. In the past, these people had simply done whatever job a farm owner had told them to do. They had never given thought to crop rotation, combining certain crops with certain livestock, paying back debt at a reasonable rate and borrowing more at the right time, selling at the right moment, and so on.

Apparently these new farmers are learning their business. As it becomes obvious that the land is going to stay in their hands, they are making the permanent additions to farm infrastructures that eventually result in profit. While many farms are in difficult financial situations, many are succeeding. When the war finally ends, it is very likely that the cooperatives will run as well as they did under their former owners.

The Successes • Despite its many problems, the land reform is seen as successful, at least by many people. The guerrillas have launched a few "final offensives," but the general population has not risen to the call. Guerrilla numbers seem to remain more or less constant.

The guerrillas' failure to inspire a popular uprising may be proving that the goal of the land reform—to weaken the base of leftist support by putting the people to work on their own land—has been achieved. Large numbers of *campesinos* are now worrying about their next harvest rather than their next meal. They have neither the time nor the desire for war.

The farmers of the cooperatives now have a direct interest in the preservation of the government. Although they still seem to support the guerrillas in their fight against the continuing abuses of the armed forces and death squads, they now have reason to worry about what a leftist government might do. Another land reform is the last thing they want!

The cooperatives that *are* working well seem to be working better than the cooperatives that were created in Nicaragua after the revolution there. One Salvadoran official explained the difference as the difference between capitalism and socialism. In Nicaragua, he said, the oligarchic ownership was replaced by government ownership. The peasant farmer still had no land, no harvest to call his own. In El Salvador, however, the peasants work on private land. As the capitalist system has always claimed, people working on their own land or in their own business tend to work harder and consequently produce more.

Shortly after the land reform was instituted, defense minister José Garcia said that the reform brought a new capitalistic spirit to El Salvador. Since more people had their own land, he said, the possibility of achieving a better life was no longer an impossible dream, as it had been under the oligarchy.

Many people disagree, however, as there has been little evidence of the poor managing to rise to the middle class. The truth is difficult to discern because of the general decline in the economy combined with the problems brought about by the war.

6

Since World War II, the free world has been wary of the domino theory. This theory suggests that the noncommunist countries of the world are like dominoes standing in a row. If one falls, it will knock down the next, which in turn will knock down the next, and so on. If unchecked, the process might eventually reach United States or European shores. To stop the process, at least one domino somewhere along the line must be fortified.

To stop the fall of dominoes as far from home as possible, the United States sent troops to South Vietnam between 1962 and 1973. But millions of dollars in economic and military aid and the deaths of more than 55,000 American soldiers failed to prevent a communist takeover. Then, in apparent accordance with the domino theory, neighboring Cambodia fell to communist invasion. Today, sporadic border skirmishes threaten Cambodia's neighbor, the next Asian domino, Thailand.

Now, almost fifteen years after the Vietnam war, people in the United States still feel the psychological wounds of that hard-learned lesson. The most powerful military force in the world had been unable to defeat a small, poorly equipped army of highly determined guerrillas. The memories of that war are now affecting the reaction of the United States to the situation in Central America, a teetering row of dominoes much closer to home.

As the domino theory could predict, the fall of Nicaragua's President Somoza in 1979 was followed by increased guerrilla activity in El Salvador. But the United States is hesitant to get involved in a fight between a repressive but pro-U.S. government and leftist guerrillas who may or may not have intentions of establishing a democracy and friendly relations with the United States.

According to the domino theory, however, any country, regardless of size, population, or natural resources, takes on great importance when it starts wavering between the influences of the two superpowers, the United States and the Soviet Union. And because El Salvador has always been a friend of the United States, our interests there are even stronger than they might be otherwise.

It would not be entirely accurate, however, to call the conflict in El Salvador a direct result of the leftist victory in Nicaragua. Salvadoran problems have been building up for a hundred years. An eruption of violence was inevitable even without such external influences as a revolution in Nicaragua or military support from other leftist countries.

Though the domino theory may not explain the cause of the conflict, the progressive expansion of revolutionary activity does give an appearance of one revolution igniting the other. As fighting moves toward the north, other Central American countries and the United States are understandably concerned.

Another Vietnam? • The phrase "another Vietnam" inevitably pops up in any debate about El Salvador. When
the first U.S. military advisers were sent to help the Salvadoran army, 200,000 protesters demonstrated in Washington, D.C. It was the largest mass demonstration since
the war in Vietnam. It was a warning that American
citizens did not want to get involved in another overseas
battle against guerrillas in their own territory.

The situations in Vietnam and El Salvador have
many similarities and differences. Vietnam had, as El
Salvador has today, a corrupt and inefficient army. Political instability in both countries led to an army that was
structured not according to ability but rather to loyalty.
Officers loyal to the current military dictator received
promotions, while those of questionable loyalty, regardless
of military skills, were left at lower ranks. In neither
country was the general population fighting to defend their
liberty, because the apparent democracies were really just
the result of fraudulent elections. And the American soldiers who went to Vietnam were far from their own country, so it was hard to equate fighting a battle in Southeast
Asia with defending the shores of North America.

But there are differences between El Salvador and
Vietnam. El Salvador is much closer to the United States.
Fighter jets could travel from El Salvador to Texas (or vice
versa) in a couple of hours instead of a couple of days. Also,
South Vietnam bordered North Vietnam, which supplied

*Many people in the United
States fear that El Salvador
will become another Vietnam
unless we cease all aid and
intervention there.*

the communist forces in the south. El Salvador has no such neighbor, though the potential exists in Nicaragua. El Salvador is also much smaller than Vietnam and does not have the monsoon rains and tropical jungles that make army maneuvers difficult. Finally, El Salvador made significant progress toward democracy during the 1980s—progress that encourages the population to defend its newfound freedom.

Langhorne Motley, former assistant secretary for inter-American affairs, discussed the Vietnam analogy in a report to Congress in 1985:

> *There are two things that the vast majority of the American people do not want in this [Central American] region: they do not want a second Cuba, and they do not want a second Vietnam. By a second Cuba, I mean the institutionalization of another well-armed communist state, this time on the mainland, supported by the Soviet Union and working actively against U.S. interests and friends in the region.*
>
> *And, by a second Vietnam, I mean a prolonged conflict involving U.S. combat troops with no clear goal and no end in sight consistent with the protection of strategic American interests.*
>
> *It is true that some Americans are concerned with one and not the other: some would risk another Vietnam to prevent another Cuba, while others are so concerned with any sign of a second Vietnam that they ignore the threat of a second Cuba. But the majority of our fellow citizens seek and will support a policy which serves our interests while preventing both a new Cuba and a new Vietnam.*

El Salvador is the United States's first opportunity to prove that it learned a lesson in Vietnam. No longer does the world's strongest military power believe that military action is the solution to peasant uprising. In El Salvador, the U.S. has been trying to approach the problem from three angles: military, democratic, and economic.

The military approach comes through military aid. During the 1980s, military aid to El Salvador declined gradually from $146 million in 1985 to about $85 million in 1989. The amount is always debated in Congress and always contingent on "good behavior" by the Salvadoran military. This aid is not enough to beef up the Salvadoran army to the point where it can launch a general attack against the guerrillas, but it is enough to keep it fighting.

The democratic approach comes through U.S. insistence that the military allow democratically elected civilians to remain in power. A military coup would mean an immediate end to all military aid. The United States also insists that the government take steps to investigate death squad killings, especially those of American church workers and land reform consultants.

The economic approach comes in the form of economic aid. Though one of the smallest countries in the western hemisphere, El Salvador has received more economic aid than any other country on this side of the world. Without this aid, the government would go bankrupt and the country would soon collapse. The guerrillas would win by default.

U.S. Economic Interests in El Salvador • El Salvador's political importance exceeds its economic importance. As a supplier of raw materials and manufactured goods, it offers little more than coffee and sugar, which are replaced easily by other sources. And El Salvador is too poor to be a significant market for U.S. goods.

There are, however, several U.S. multinational corporations doing business in El Salvador. Some U.S. manufacturing plants are there because workers' wages are substantially lower than in the United States. Others are involved only with the sales and maintenance of their products. The total U.S. investment is about $100 million—not much in relation to the U.S. economy as a whole but of some significance to the companies involved. Few if any of them would go bankrupt over the loss of their interests in El Salvador, but none of them would like to lose what they have invested there.

When José Duarte's junta nationalized the banks, it arranged to reimburse foreign banks to avoid loss of investment. Other businesses worry that a complete leftist takeover might not result in such fair treatment. Leftist takeovers in Cuba, Vietnam, and Angola have brought about the nationalization of many or all foreign industries, often with little or no reimbursement.

If the potential economic loss to U.S. companies is small, however, the potential political loss of El Salvador could range from irritating to disastrous. A leftist government might be merely unfriendly to the United States, or it might go to the extreme of becoming an overseas base for Cuba or the Soviet Union.

Cuban Activity in Latin America • Since 1959, when Fidel Castro overthrew a rightist dictatorship in Cuba and established a communist government, Cuba has been exporting communist beliefs. As Castro proudly admits, Cuba has been carrying out communist subversion in Latin America for twenty-one years and it is finally beginning to pay off.

Cuba occupies a strategic location among dozens of countries in the Caribbean area that are economically weak enough to inspire lower-class revolution and militarily weak enough to allow guerrillas to get a foothold in the jungles and mountains. Some of these countries are islands no more than a hundred miles (160 km) across. In others, leftist guerrillas are active. El Salvador and Guatemala are the most serious examples, and Colombia and Honduras are also experiencing problems.

So far, Cuban troops have not fought alongside Latin American guerrillas. There is little doubt, though, that Cuba has been secretly supplying arms and advisers to the leftists it would like to see running governments. Guerrilla leaders from Nicaragua, El Salvador, and Guatemala have traveled to Havana for training, conferences, and moral support.

Cuban activities in Latin America directly affect U.S. policy there. When Cuban aid, which often originates in the Soviet Union, consists of teachers, doctors, engineers, and other nonmilitary advisers, the United States sees little reason to interfere. Such aid has been sent to the islands of Grenada and Santa Lucia and to the new leftist government of Nicaragua. But when the aid to rebels consists of machine guns, rocket launchers, and ammunition, the United States responds by giving the same kind of aid to the nations' governments.

Past U.S. Policies in Latin America • For almost 160 years, United States policy in Latin America has been based on principles set forth by President James Monroe in 1823. Known as the Monroe Doctrine, this declaration recognized the newly won independence of all Latin American countries and stated that any attempt by European powers to interfere in their free development would be considered a threat to the peace and security of the United States. Such interference, therefore, would constitute enough reason for the United States to take appropriate action.

The United States has used the Monroe Doctrine to justify its actions on numerous occasions, notably in the Cuban missile crisis of 1962. But the United States has also acted in secrecy in an effort to secure friendly governments in Latin America, as it did in Guatemala in 1954 and in Chile in the early 1970s.

As the self-appointed protector of democracy in Latin America, the United States has often appeared to act chiefly in support of its own economic and political interests, without concern for the best interests of the local population or the political processes of the countries in which it was intervening. Consequently, the United States is widely regarded as arrogant and heavy-handed in its dealings with Latin American governments.

John F. Kennedy was one of the few U.S. presidents who tried to reverse this view of the United States. Kennedy knew that the area was susceptible to communist subversion. In an attempt to alleviate the potential causes of trouble, he declared war on Latin American poverty. In the 1960s, through the Alliance for Progress, millions of dollars in assistance were spent to develop Latin American economies and raise the standard of living to reduce the allure of communist promises.

The Alliance for Progress was only moderately successful, however. Much aid money remained in the pockets of the dictators, and in many cases, a country's upper class used the aid to develop the industries they themselves owned. Little aid actually filtered down to the lower classes.

In El Salvador, too, the upper-class oligarchy used the Alliance for its own purposes. To qualify for the aid, the Alliance required that the government establish a minimum wage law. El Salvador did so, but landowners used the law as an excuse to stop providing free meals for their farm workers. Forced to buy their meals from the landowners, the workers found themselves taking home less pay than before.

President Carter's Human Rights Policy • In the years following President Kennedy's death, U.S. foreign policy was preoccupied with the war in Southeast Asia; Latin America was largely ignored. By the time Jimmy Carter took office in 1977, however, Central America, especially Nicaragua, was rumbling with imminent eruption.

From the beginning of his administration, President Carter based his foreign policy on a nation's respect for human rights. Soviet-style governments are infamous for abusing such human rights as freedom from arrest and torture as well as the freedoms of speech, press, and religion. But rightist dictators are rarely any more respectful of their citizens.

During the civil war in Nicaragua, the United States had no desire to support the government of President Somoza, who had never shown any respect for human rights. The conflict in Nicaragua was waged against an intolerable dictatorship. It was fought to eliminate a cruel and corrupt government, not to install a communist government.

As it became increasingly apparent that the Nicaraguan leftists might win the war, the United States felt even less inclined to support Somoza. Supporting the loser of a battle hurts future relations with the winner. On the other hand, supporting the leftists might be equally unwise should their new government turn out to be a Cuban-style dictatorship with a policy of exporting revolution to neighboring countries by supplying guerrillas with arms and other aid. These factors, combined with Somoza's human rights abuses and the U.S. fear of another "Vietnam," persuaded the United States to avoid getting involved in Nicaragua.

When Somoza's government fell in 1979 and a junta of guerrilla leaders assumed control of the country, the United States was cautious in sending aid to the new Nicaraguan government. Although leftist, it would be acceptable if it respected human rights, remained democratic, and did not become overly friendly with Cuba and the Soviet Union. When the junta, in desperate need of funds to rebuild the war-ravaged country, accepted aid and advisers—mostly nonmilitary—from Cuba, the United States limited its aid to a loan of $75 million.

Gradually, during the last year of President Carter's administration, it became apparent that Nicaragua was not going to be a perfect democracy. Dissidents were arrested, and an antigovernment newspaper was shut down.

As the violence in El Salvador grew worse in 1979, the United States knew it had to find some way to prevent "another Nicaragua" in which a leftist victory would lead to an anti-U.S. government. But at the same time, the United States did not want to get involved in "another Vietnam," another long war fighting guerrillas in their own territory.

The U.S. ambassador to El Salvador, Robert E. White, who had taken office just after the 1979 coup that had ousted President Romero, believed that land reform offered the best solution for El Salvador. It would fit well with President Carter's human rights policy and at the same time would take away the guerrillas' base of support among the *campesinos*. He vigorously opposed military intervention, believing it would give the guerrillas all the more reason to fight.

Ambassador White was branded a socialist by the Salvadoran oligarchy, which opposed his plan, and conservatives in the United States saw his plan for land reform as a surrender to leftist demands. They believed that the only answer was military support of the junta. A show of force would tell the world that America was ready to fight fire with fire.

President Carter, however, decided to try White's idea. By using U.S. aid as a lever, he hoped to force the junta to begin respecting human rights and to carry out the land reforms that had been under discussion for more than a decade. Ideally, El Salvador would become a model for the rest of Latin America—an alternative to communist revolution and the dictatorship that seemed inevitably to follow.

Over the next year, however, the situation deteriorated, in spite of the effort to begin land reform. As we have seen, the military members of the junta paid no attention to the demands of the civilian members. Both sides continued to fight and to die. By the end of 1980, the year's death toll had reached almost 13,000. Among the deaths at the end of 1980 were four that brought the conflict in El Salvador even closer to the consciousness of people in the United States.

On December 2, four American women were kidnapped while driving into San Salvador from the airport. Three were nuns—Dorothy Kazel, Ita Ford, and Maura Clarke—and one was a young missionary, Jean Donovan. Their burned van was found beside the road the next day. Reports of machine-gun fire during the night led peasants to a shallow grave where they found the bodies of the women. All four had been shot, and two showed signs of rape.

Though accusations flew in all directions, the evidence pointed to the rightists. The bullets were of the type supplied by the United States to the Salvadoran army, and the style of killing was typical of rightist death squads. Likewise, the target of the attack—church workers helping the poor—was one aimed at only by the rightists. At first the Salvadoran government denied any responsibility and

The kidnapping and deaths of four American women
—three nuns and a missionary—in 1980 brought
the conflict in El Salvador home to America.
Five former Salvadoran National Guards were
accused of the killings and brought to trial.

blamed the guerrillas, but they later changed the story, saying that the women had run a roadblock. As a result of the incident, the United States immediately banned all aid to El Salvador until a thorough investigation could be carried out.

It was at this time that the Salvadoran guerrillas, knowing that Ronald Reagan would become president on January 20, 1981, and that the Salvadoran government now lacked U.S. support, launched what they called their "final offensive." They hoped to be so close to victory by the time Reagan took office that it would be too late for a tougher U.S. policy to stop them.

The failure of the offensive, which has been described in Chapter 5, was important to U.S. policy for two reasons. Politically, it revealed that the general population did not totally support the guerrillas, and militarily, it gave the United States good reason to lift its ban on aid to El Salvador. Just before leaving office, President Carter approved $15 million in military aid to El Salvador. This was the first provision of lethal weapons to that country since 1977.

New Policies in the Reagan Administration • Ronald Reagan had campaigned for president with a promise to restore international respect for the United States by directly confronting the advance of communism. Within one week of his inauguration, the new president demonstrated his determination to put his policies into effect in El Salvador. He was supported in this action by his newly appointed secretary of state, Alexander Haig, who shared the president's desire to take a strong stand against communist influence in the world.

Calling the Salvadoran conflict "a textbook case of indirect armed aggression by communist powers," Reagan and Haig asked Congress to increase military aid to El

Salvador to $64 million, including provision for fifty-six U.S. military advisers.

The new direction in U.S. policy necessitated a change in ambassadors to El Salvador. President Carter's appointee, Robert White, was replaced by Frederic Chapin, who would serve as chargé d'affaires until a qualified ambassador could be found for this difficult post. Chapin was a career diplomat who recently had been working with the Defense Department on plans for a military-aid project for El Salvador. His appointment was considered an indication of the seriousness of the new U.S. policy of seeking a military solution to the Salvadoran conflict.

At the same time that the Reagan administration moved to bolster the Salvadoran government, it cut off all aid to Nicaragua. The decision to break with Nicaragua came amid accusations from the State Department that weapons donated by communist powers were being shipped to Nicaragua and from there by land, sea, and air to El Salvador.

This accusation marked a serious turning point in the Salvadoran conflict. It meant that the civil war had expanded, in the perception of many observers, from an internal conflict between local government and guerrillas into a conflict between the two superpowers—the United States and the Soviet Union.

The evidence of Soviet influence was contained in documents that had been captured from Salvadoran guerrillas. These documents revealed specific information about numbers and types of arms and how they found their way to El Salvador from the four corners of the world. The documents were published in a State Department white paper entitled "Communist Interference in El Salvador." The white paper (as it is commonly called) reported that 200 tons of arms and ammunition had been channeled through Cuba and Nicaragua into El Salvador just before the guerrilla offensive of January 1981. To disguise the Soviet Union as the supplier of the weapons and make it appear that the guerrillas had bought them on the black market, many of the weapons were of German, Belgian, and Israeli manufacture. Some were U.S. M-16s captured during the Vietnam war. The report also claimed that various communist countries, including Vietnam, Ethiopia, Hungary, and East Germany, had promised to send another 600 tons of arms, and that Cuba was training the Salvadoran guerrillas.

Many journalists and various antiwar organizations who examined the white paper reported that the evidence was by no means conclusive. The translations were inaccurate and the facts, dates, and names were inconsistent. In one case, a captured document written in Spanish had been a "request" for arms, whereas the English translation made it a "promise" of arms. The white paper brought the Reagan administration into its first controversy. When its evidence was used to justify increasing aid and sending advisers, protests were heard across the United States and in Europe.

In Washington, over 20,000 people demonstrated in opposition to U.S. involvement in El Salvador, the largest political demonstration since the Vietnam War. Among the protesters were congressmen, labor leaders, college professors, and people from some 700 different organizations, many of them religious. Thousands of other people joined the protest by writing to newspaper editors and government representatives. A senator in California reported that letters regarding El Salvador were running 100 to 1 against U.S. involvement. Many protesters saw intervention in El Salvador as the beginning of another Vietnam—first arms, then advisers, then troops to protect the advisers, and then whole army divisions.

President Reagan countered the protests by emphatically denying that the United States would ever engage in combat in El Salvador. His only purpose was to support the politically moderate junta in its attempts to make land reform succeed. He stressed that the United States would tolerate neither a coup by the rightists nor a military victory by the leftists; either occurrence would mean a cutoff of all U.S. aid.

A Report to Congress • In January 1981, just as U.S. policy in El Salvador was undergoing a change of direction, three members of the House of Representatives— Gerry Studds, Barbara Mikulski, and Robert Edgar— traveled to Central America on a fact-finding mission. They wanted to talk with Salvadoran government officials, guerrilla leaders, and refugees. Because the State Department asked them not to enter El Salvador, where their safety could not be guaranteed, they conducted interviews in San José, Costa Rica, and in Honduras at the Salvadoran border.

From political spokesmen, the representatives heard complaints of military control of the government. From refugees fleeing into Honduras, they heard stories of horrendously violent acts committed by the military with the intent of intimidating those who might support the guerrillas. Junta member José Morales Ehrlich, not surprisingly, urged U.S. support of his government as the only alternative to the extremes of right and left. Yet Ruben Zamorro, a former Christian Democratic cabinet member of the first junta who became part of the Democratic Revolutionary Front (a coalition of leftist organizations), described the land reform as a public-relations device without significance as long as the military was in charge.

On the Honduran–El Salvador border, Representatives Mikulski and Edgar tape-recorded tales of atrocity told by refugees. In several cases, the military had bombed villages with artillery, shot at the residents with machine guns from helicopters, and then burned all the houses. Anyone caught in the village, including women and young children, was killed. In several cases, babies were tortured in order to force mothers to reveal the location of their husbands or sons. One refugee reported the rape of children as young as eight. Dismemberment, intended to spread general terror and fear, was common.

According to the report of the representatives, only the military was involved in attacks against unarmed people. Leftists attacked villages only to assassinate ORDEN members or army patrols too small to defend themselves.

On the basis of their findings, Representatives Studds, Mikulski, and Edgar made the following recommendations for U.S. policy:

> *The United States should terminate all military assistance because the armed forces are operating independently of responsible civilian control.*
>
> *U.S. economic assistance for land reform should be suspended because corruption caused by the military makes it unlikely that the funds are usefully allocated.*
>
> *Congress should investigate the killing of six Americans and the disappearance of another because it appears that the government was involved in each case.*
>
> *The United States should reexamine its policy toward El Salvador and all of Central America because the policies of the past do not deal with the reality of the present situation.*

An East-West or a North-South Conflict? • Different opinions about the conflict in El Salvador are often the result of different ways of understanding the conflict. Some people see it as an East-West conflict. "East" refers to the nondemocratic communist powers, especially the Soviet Union. "West" refers to the democracies of the United States and western Europe. "North" refers to the relatively wealthy "First World" countries of the Northern Hemisphere. "South" refers to the relatively poor "Third World" nations of the Southern Hemisphere.

Those who see the conflict in El Salvador as an East-West battle feel that the rebellion is inspired by the Soviet Union as part of a global political contest to gain allies and territories for military bases. The role of the West in this contest is to defend the countries that are friendly to the United States. The solution, according to those who see the conflict as an East-West battle, is the military defeat of the insurgent forces.

Others feel the conflict is between the wealthy Northern Hemisphere countries and the poorer countries to the south. They feel that much of the poverty in the Third World is caused by the "imperialistic" powers of the First World. By "imperialistic," they mean the policies that began with European countries controlling New World colonies. These policies, they say, continue until today, but in a different form. Today, the wealthier nations exert financial power over the poorer countries, forcing them to sell their raw materials and manufactured products at low prices. To maintain a large and cheap working class in Third World nations, the First World governments use military power, financial aid, and secret operations to keep rightist dictators in power. The solution to the North-South conflict, they say, is to end the dictatorships and help the impoverished lower classes raise their standard of living.

The truth is not clear-cut on either side. Probably both opinions are partially right. Certainly there exists a division of wealth between rich and poor nations. The

Soviet Union has tried to take advantage of that difference, and the United States has used the Marines and the CIA to keep friendly but nondemocratic governments from being overthrown by leftists.

These two ways of seeing the conflict in El Salvador were very apparent in two televised speeches given in 1983. President Reagan, who held office from 1981 to 1989, was advocating a strong response to leftist guerrilla activity in Central America. In 1983, when Congress hesitated to send El Salvador the aid he requested, President Reagan called a joint session of Congress so he could explain the problem as he saw it. Since it was broadcast on television, he had to allow Democratic senator Christopher Dodd of Connecticut to offer an opposing view.

President Reagan stressed that El Salvador was close to important shipping lanes, including the Panama Canal. He also pointed out the progress that the Salvadoran government had made in human rights. Elections had given El Salvador its first democratically elected government in fifty years. The land reform had distributed land to almost half a million peasants who had never before hoped to own land. It would not be right, Reagan said, to allow communists to use violence to end all this progress.

President Reagan outlined four American goals in Central America:

> *To reverse the centuries of dictatorship and human rights abuses, the United States would, from then on, do what it could to support democracy, social reform and liberty.*

> *To counter the economic problems of the region and the guerrilla economic sabotage in El Salvador, the United States would support economic development by providing loans and economic aid much more than military aid.*

Despite the threat of revolutions inspired and financed by Nicaragua and Cuba, the United States would never send U.S. troops to Central America.

The United States would support dialogues and negotiations among the countries and forces in Central America.

Concluding his speech, President Reagan said that the situation was critical, that the security of the United States was at stake. He then asked the Congress for $600 million in aid for Central America—one-tenth of what Americans spent on video games in 1983.

Senator Dodd, speaking on behalf of the Democratic party after the president's speech, saw the conflict from a different angle. After affirming that the United States could never accept another Marxist government in Central America or Soviet bases in Central America, he went on to redefine the problem.

The causes of the conflict, said Dodd, were the rightist dictators, the hopeless poverty, the death squads, the general injustice. Under such conditions, rebellions were bound to erupt, with or without the help of Cuba or the Soviet Union. A military solution was as wrong in Central America as it was in Vietnam.

Senator Dodd said that the solution had to be social, not military. The United States had to make violent revolution preventable by making peaceful revolution possi-

One of fifty-five military advisers the Reagan administration sent to the war-torn country

ble. The government of El Salvador would have to put a stop to the death squads and to push ahead with the land reform if it wanted aid from the United States.

Dollars for Democracy • Congress has been keeping a close watch on the progress of democracy and respect for human rights in El Salvador. Money has been the U.S. weapon against both communism and criminal government in El Salvador. Between 1980 and 1989, the United States sent over $3.5 billion to El Salvador, an average of about $14 each second. After 1984, aid averaged $1.1 million per day, subsidizing half of El Salvador's federal budget. Without this aid, the Salvadoran government would surely run out of money—and ammunition—in a matter of weeks.

Congress made it clear that this aid depends on good behavior. A military coup against Duarte would mean an immediate end to all military and economic support. Congress also demanded that the president of the United States report twice a year to confirm that El Salvador was carrying out a land reform, that the murders of two U.S. land reform advisers were being investigated, and that death squad activities and political killings were being reduced.

Issues for the United States • Because the outcome of the conflict in El Salvador is so important to the United States, and because U.S. foreign policy directly influences the course of events in El Salvador, the crisis in this Central American country raises many questions for policy makers. It is also important for U.S. citizens to understand the problems and questions their nation faces in El Salvador.

The possibility of U.S. military intervention is probably the biggest issue confronting officials. Under what circumstances might the United States need to send troops

In addition to military aid, the U.S. has other influences in El Salvador. There are many programs designed to employ idle workmen and keep them from joining the guerrilla movement.

there? To prevent a leftist military victory? To counteract Cuban or Soviet involvement? To prevent further human rights abuses in the event of a military coup?

How should U.S. foreign aid be used to influence the situation? The complete withdrawal of aid would increase the country's poverty and perhaps even cause the collapse of the economy. Yet aid without human rights restrictions might encourage the extreme right to continue its death squad tactics and discourage free elections. Do human rights become less important in the context of a war? Should stopping communism take priority over the elimination of human rights abuses?

The question of foreign aid raises still another question: What sort of government is it helping? Is El Salvador still a military state where civilian leaders are only puppets of army officers?

As guerrilla fighting increases in other Central American countries, Americans must ask themselves how it can be stopped. Is land reform a reasonable compromise between oligarchic repression and communist revolution? Will breaking the oligarchic grip on a country's economy bring stability? In El Salvador, although the land reform did not stop the guerrillas, it did seem to diminish some of their popular support. Would a similar plan have similar effects elsewhere?

These are not easy issues. Government officials debate them, officially and unofficially, every day. Millions of dollars and thousands of lives depend on their conclusions. Ultimately, the issue concerns not only El Salvador, but the future of democracy in the Western Hemisphere.

7

THE FUTURE OF EL SALVADOR

By 1989, neither the left nor the right had gained an advantage in the conflict in El Salvador. In fact, little territory had changed hands in several years. United States and Salvadoran officials agree that it is going to be a long war, and that probably neither side would ever win a clear-cut victory. Meanwhile, people die. As in all wars, civilians suffer far more casualties than those who are fighting.

But even a stalemate is a kind of victory for the guerrillas. As they gradually destroy the economy and frustrate attempts at democracy, they wear down the ability of the government to govern. If serious and productive negotiations ever take place, the guerrillas are sure to exact concessions from the government.

As we have seen in Chapter One, the current strife in El Salvador stems from the landlessness and widespread unemployment caused by overpopulation, from a lower class rebelling against half a century of military rule and social injustice, and from the hopelessness generated by illiteracy and the lack of alternatives to migrant labor and eternal poverty.

Industrialization: A Possible Solution • Because the land alone cannot possibly provide enough food and jobs for 5 million people, El Salvador will have to turn to industrialization as a solution to its economic problems. Manufacturing produces more money on less land. The increased production and exportation of manufactured goods would provide the country with money to import the food and other goods it needs to raise the general standard of living. Permanent jobs in industry would allow each successive generation to provide a better starting point for the advancement of the next. As workers find alternatives to farm labor, landowners will be forced to pay higher wages. In this way, El Salvador could rise from its deep poverty.

No such progress is possible, however, in a country whose workers are illiterate. Manufacturing calls for educated workers. If they can't read, it is almost impossible to train them. Many have limited intelligence due to malnutrition in childhood. In a world where many manufacturing jobs demand a working knowledge of computers, a factory cannot afford to begin to train workers by teaching them how to tie their boots. But if these workers have never owned shoes before, that's where the training has to start.

Similarly, a country cannot advance if its people are unhealthy or on the verge of starvation. Likewise, if a small, wealthy group of people can disregard the law while less wealthy people have no access to the system of justice, the society will not function smoothly or peacefully.

All of this adds up to the fact that no military victory or any end to the fighting will solve El Salvador's problems. The changes have to be broad and deep, cutting through all levels of society. In many ways, El Salvador has to go through the same social, economic, and political changes that Europe and North America have gone through since the beginning of the Industrial Revolution. This will not happen quickly or easily.

But the growth of democracy will make it possible for the country to change. Today, only the fragile framework of democracy exists. But as that democracy becomes stronger, it will lay the foundations of long-term peace and prosperity. The question is whether extreme rightists or extreme leftists will succeed in destroying what has been built at such tragic expense.

As the conflict continues, Americans continue to question the importance of the situation and its possible outcome. Is the Salvadoran government worth supporting? Is communism a real threat to the security of Central America and the United States? How much American money is Salvadoran democracy worth? What is the best way to end the conflict and solve the problems that created it? If communist guerrillas ever seem to be winning the conflict, should the United States send troops?

The situation in El Salvador is similar to situations in other Latin American countries, especially those in Central America. Military governments, wealthy landowners, impoverished masses, leftists calling for revolution, rightists using force to preserve their system of law, order and economics—these problems exist throughout the region. It is likely that they will someday suffer the same problems that El Salvador has today. It would be nice if we could find a solution to these problems before they erupt in war.

A top State Department official emphasized the importance of these questions, saying " . . . the decisive battle for Central America is under way in El Salvador." It is, indeed, a key point in regional, if not global, politics.

*It is still too soon to know how President Bush
and his administration stand on the conflict
in El Salvador. One clue, however, may be the
meeting held between Salvadoran President Alfredo
Cristiani and Vice-President Dan Quayle, rather
than with the president, in the spring of 1989.*

With so much foreign influence surrounding such a small country, El Salvador's Archbishop Rivera y Damas feels that the conflict has expanded beyond the control of the Salvadoran people. In a particularly poignant remark, he said that "foreign countries, in their zeal to dominate the world, will supply the weapons, while Salvadorans supply the bodies."

FOR FURTHER READING

For an inside look at El Salvador, read *El Salvador: Embassy Under Attack* (Vantage Press, 1981). For the closest possible view of contemporary El Salvador, read José Napoleón Duarte's *Duarte: My Story* (Putnam, 1986). Richard A. Nuccio's *What's Wrong, Who's Right in Central America* (Roosevelt Center for American Policy Studies) has clear and comprehensive information about the situation in El Salvador and in neighboring countries.

Since the situation in El Salvador is always changing, newspaper and magazine articles are the best source of up-to-date information. *Time, Newsweek, Nation, Foreign Affairs, Foreign Policy, Latin American Perspectives,* and the *Journal of Latin American Studies* carry good articles. The *New York Times,* the *Washington Post,* and the *Christian Science Monitor* very often report on the situation.

International organizations publishing reports include the Organization of American States, in Washington, D.C.; the Unitarian Universalist Service Committee, in Boston; OXFAM, in Boston; Amnesty International, in New York; CISPES (Committee in Solidarity for the People of El Salvador), in Washington; the Religious Task Force, in Washington; and the U.S. State Department. Your congressional representative may have information that the Congress has used to make U.S. policy decisions.

INDEX

ABOUT THE AUTHOR

*Glenn Alan Cheney, a free-lance writer and
an adjunct professor at Fairfield University
in Connecticut, has a B.A. in philosophy and
an M.A. in communication, both from that
same university.*

*After traveling throughout Latin America,
he spent several years living in São Paulo
and Belo Horizonte, Brazil, where he had a
company that taught English and wrote reports
for Brazilian companies.*

As a free lance (listed in Contemporary
Authors), *he has written nine books, several
radio dramas, part of a handbook of business
terms, many newspaper and magazine articles,
and countless reports, manuals, and public
relations materials for corporations.*

*He currently lives in Milford, Connecticut,
with his wife, Solange, and son, Ian.*

DATE DUE

		MAY 0 7 2003	
GAYLORD			PRINTED IN U.S.A.